Studies in Media Management
A. William Bluem, General Editor 1968–1974

CASE STUDIES IN BROADCAST MANAGEMENT

Studies in Media Management

BROADCAST MANAGEMENT
Radio-Television,
First Edition by Ward L. Quaal and Leo A. Martin
Second Edition, Revised and Enlarged
by Ward L. Quaal and James A. Brown

CLASSROOM TELEVISION
New Frontiers in ITV
by George N. Gordon

CASE STUDIES IN BROADCAST MANAGEMENT
Second Edition, Revised and Enlarged
by Howard W. Coleman

THE MOVIE BUSINESS
American Film Industry Practice
Edited by A. William Bluem and Jason E. Squire

THE CHANGING MAGAZINE
Trends in Readership and Management
by Roland E. Wolseley

FILM LIBRARY TECHNIQUES
Principles of Administration
by Helen P. Harrison

THE FILM INDUSTRIES
*Practical Business/Legal Problems
in Production, Distribution and Exhibition*
Second Edition, Revised and Enlarged
by Michael F. Mayer

AMERICAN NEWSPAPERS IN THE 1970s
by Ernest C. Hynds

Case Studies in Broadcast Management: Radio and Television

Second Edition, Revised and Enlarged

by

Howard W. Coleman

Communication Arts Books

Hastings House, Publishers

New York 10016

Copyright © 1978, 1970 by Howard W. Coleman
All rights reserved. No part of this publication may be reproduced, stored in a retrieval system, or transmitted, in any form or by any means, electronic, mechanical, photocopying, recording or otherwise, without the prior permission of the copyright owner or the publishers.

Library of Congress Cataloging in Publication Data
Coleman, Howard W
   Case studies in broadcast management.
   (Studies in media management) (Communication arts books)
   Bibliography: p.
   1. Broadcasting—United States—Management—Case studies.   I. Title.
HE8689.8.C58   1978   658'.91'384540722   77-18981
ISBN 0-8038-1220-5
ISBN 0-8038-1221-3 pbk.
Published simultaneously in Canada by
Copp Clark Ltd., Toronto
Printed in the United States of America

For Joan

CONTENTS

Introduction by Kenneth A. Mills   9
Preface   11
Acknowledgements   17
Suggested Readings   19
A Writer's Opinion   21

Part I: CASE STUDY PROBLEMS

1. *Television Violence: Are the kiddies being warped, or woofed—or just laughing at the attention?*   25

   A cross-section of relevant quotes introduces this problem as it relates to the responsible local TV operator

2. *Station Revenue and the Station Manager*   35

   Inflation; stagflation; the profit structure—planning for economy in operation *and* increased revenue

3. *The Radio Audience: Where is it, how do we acquire more?*   43

   A cross-section of how stations with various program formats fare in large, medium and small markets prefaces this problem of how a middle-of-the-road station looks to a brighter identity and a more stable future

4. *Paid Religion: Do You or Don't You?*   51

   A puzzling policy problem: quick money but maybe community relations problems as well

5. *A Stitch in Time Saves Seven*   55

   The late evening news-weather-sports period: a rating weakness, and what to do?

7. *Your Horse for my Cow: Barter in Local Television*   149

Not new, but in a resurgence, the barter concept may serve to breathe new life into stations below the Top 40 or so. Can it serve, or does it shortstop national spot income and obfuscate true income and dollar value in the medium?

8. *Enhancing the News*   152

"Bang-bang, boom-boom, no!" But where can we draw a line in making the news more dramatic without special effects?

INTRODUCTION FOR CASE STUDIES SECOND EDITION

Howard Coleman has the effrontery in this text to imply that good old fashioned *literacy,* coupled with a wide knowledge of the major thrusts of communications writing and technology on civilization, might just be more important tools for the broadcast management executive than a successful record as a time salesman.

If this isn't outrageous enough, he reaches for old Roy Rogers stories to make a point. He goes back to the "earliest hearing on TV violence and children" to underscore the ineffectual throbbings of so many earnest groups as they grope with this issue 25 years later.

Coleman cites *New Yorker* cartoons; doesn't hesitate to demythologize the concept of "radio—the flexible medium, always ready." The characters who people many of his chapters—Butterfield, Samuels, Blodgett, Starrs, Trent—are real and all-too-recognizable types in the world of broadcasting. We have both known them, sometimes in the same place at the same time!

Here then is a generous slice of broadcasting as it exists: realistic but not cynical, and with the strong suggestion that through recognition of the present state of the art better things may happen.

> KENNETH A. MILLS
> Vice President, The Katz Agency, Inc.
> New York

PREFACE

In 1968 the team of distinguished broadcast executive Ward L. Quaal of the WGN Companies and the late Leo Martin, chairman of the Television-Radio Department at Michigan State University, produced *Broadcast Management: Radio + Television,* a comprehensive and durable text that received wide recognition and usage.

In 1970, in an attempt to complement that effort with practical, in-class discussion materials, I produced *Case Studies in Broadcast Management*—an effort that seems to have been well received. Lest that seem to be puffery on the part of this author, let it be known for the record that the original Quaal-Martin text has gone through eight printings; *Case Studies* achieved its third printing in mid-1976.

In that Quaal-Martin text the authors quoted Charles Brower of Batten, Barton, Durstine and Osborne: "There is no business that so thoroughly punishes the amateur. In a business such as ours, where boys and girls becomes men and women rapidly, you have to have a lot more than heart. You have to have that—plus responsibility, judgment and understanding."

To this basic subject of *Broadcast Management* this writer once assembled a profile of the fiscally-responsible, working manager in response to the assigned topic of a speech before a business luncheon club, an opus titled "How were you so lucky to get into this kind of work?"

Among other things, I said that the management of a radio and/or TV station demanded that you be:

- a *legal expert*, with a Solomon-type approach toward "equal time" and "fairness doctrine" questions and the demands of union shop stewards;
- a *father figure*, in dealing with the problems and actions of salesmen—and sometimes sales managers;
- a *child psychologist*, in treatment of the woes of talent—working under the theme of "Talent is/are children";
- a kindly-but-firm *policeman*, making sure that all the kiddies in your employ are doing what they are supposed to do, with no truants hiding in the alley;
- a *minor prophet*, shepherding the flock toward greener pastures—even though it may mean walking behind them and kicking their rumps;
- a *citizen of the community*, eager to join and to work with everything from the Better Business Bureau to the save-the-purple-grackle campaign;
- a Januslike *Santa Claus-Scrooge figure*, giving forth the aura of dispensing largesse with a free hand while at the same time keeping a close eye on the profit-and-loss statements;
- a *Boy Scout*—and here Quaal and Martin have said it well: "One might as well cite the Scout law for its pertinence and value judgments";
- And where all else fails, a *chaplain*, equipped in the military sense of the word with a heart-shaped punch for indenting the cards of the hapless of the world who parade before your desk!

But broadcasting is a fast-moving industry. In 1976 Dr. James A. Brown, S.J., former chairman of the Radio-Television Department at the University of Detroit and of the Telecommunications Department at the University of Southern California, joined with Ward Quaal to produce a second edition of *Broadcast Management: Radio + Television*—an extensively revised and enlarged version of the first text.

In that major revision, Quaal and Brown offer this thought:

> Intelligent and responsible management cannot be realized by uncreative and imitative methods. There must be a considerable evaluation of the potential that generally has not been put to use in broadcasting. Few station managers

Preface

have achieved the genuine stature their calling makes possible. Such accomplishment depends upon the manner in which the true executive approaches his task and the results that he produces. Collectively, the various instances of achievement can change the image of broadcasting.

Some notes on this second edition of *Case Studies in Broadcast Management: Radio + Television.*

This text expanded as the galleys of the Quaal-Brown text came through: the hope is to continue to supply in-class discussion materials that are timely and in balance with the Quaal-Brown emphasis. In *no way* are these materials offered to be a chapter-by-chapter workbook in line with that text.

A note of special emphasis: Response from the groves of academe, in the five-plus years since the first publication of *Case Studies,* has occasionally indicated that one or another of the studies was obsolecsent, if not obsolete. In other words, *the problem no longer exists.*

This may well be true, in the market where that respondent lives, or in his or her own experience.

But to this the writer and publisher reply: The case studies encompass a broad, diversified and very new industry. It is well worth it that the student contemplate what *has* happened as well as *what is happening* and as well, *what is about to happen.* Some of the problems that may have been pertinent in the lower end of the "Top 100" markets no longer apply; however, these situations may be of top yes-or-no decision at the 200th market level.

Text Organization

The text is in three parts: Part I—*Case Study Problems*—offers detailed exploration of broadcast areas in which the problems are serious, the resolutions far-reaching and properly described as long-range in planning and resolution.

Part II—*Case Study Profiles*—outlines in briefer forms the kinds of problems that are for the most part short-ranged and capable of a solution that does *not* commit long-range involvement or capital investment, either in people or equipment.

Part III—*Situation Statements*—a new section added to the first edition of *Case Studies,* which suggests that the student is ready to construct case studies, to seek out and find the problem in a given situation—possibly, to borrow from Murphy's Law ("If anything can go wrong, it will"), to anticipate the *consequences* of a decision or line of action.

Or the results of inertia.

. . .

In many areas of industry and association work the "project description" technique is being used as a bible. A tightly-knit format, or series of formats, it forces the planner, the budgeter, the department head, to put on paper all of the problems (or *situations*), aims, goals, procedures, costs—and to establish a graded scale of priorities for action.

This is anethema to many oldtimers. "I've always done it that way," one grumbles. "Got piles of paper on my desk that say *urgent, do it yesterday, important, first of the month,* and *hold. Hold* means ignore it and maybe it'll go away!"

But to the new management breed, charting in orderly fashion from 1 through 10, project descriptions and similar models are the very lifeblood without which nothing can happen. It's an updated form of the domino theory of 1960's geopolitics—one false move and the entire structure topples. Or, in business phraseology, alter any element of the over-all system and all other elements of that system are in turn altered, perhaps weakened and/or damaged; possibly the entire system is toppled.

Can the slide rule and the economic micrometer be applied to a subject so ephemeral as broadcasting? On the network level NBC has passed through management planning phases of this sort and survived. In 1958, under parent RCA aegis, NBC sent 160 middle management executives to an "Advanced Management School" at Princeton, with the avowed statement (and much publicity) to claim that this was the way of the future in long range management strength and growth.

Most of those aging students labored mightily, with the promise of veepee stripes just around the corner. Yet in August of the same year the network had fired 82 of the 160: this was short range management planning that had to do with making a new record target net income "for the General" by December 31!

Since these people were able to take their new skills with them to other broadcast employers, the project was highly successful in that it provided superior management training—the only questionable aspect being that over half of it went to the competition. At an

Preface

average cost of $4,000 per student, this was a major NBC/RCA gift to the industry.

On the local broadcast level there is little time to make models of long-range projects, and precious few moments to play dominoes. Yet it is a business far beyond the sale of hamburgers "two-for-one-on-Mondays" or the giving away of glasses with every eight gallons purchased. Regulatory agencies and Congressional task forces are on the eyepiece end of the microscope. Religious and public service groups are peering through the large ends of denominational and/or partisan telescopes.

Local station operation does need thought; it does need planning. *Can* this thought and planning be channeled efficiently and economically for local station use? The heart of the project description technique is in the *situation analysis,* wherein a specific problem is isolated, described in clinical detail, strobe-lighted and centrifuge-spun, and procedures subsequently suggested.

Granted that the broad scope of situation analysis is too far-ranging for this purpose, I will seize editorial prerogative and submit a modified term—*situation statement.*

Is this too strenuous a technique to contemplate? I think not; in our town the merchants have an annual "Follies Week" in July, and dump out at ten-cents-on-the-dollar all the dubious merchandise stocked by emotion rather than logic during the past year and proved to be unsaleable.

But July is a marginal month for most broadcasters, and the dusty inventory of white plastic boots with pink sequins and yo-yos that glow in the dark won't move at any price—in local radio and TV.

And, I submit, the commercial broadcaster must be warier, most selective, more cautious—more *anticipatory,* if you will—than his fellow chamber of commerce members in the white goods and variety merchandise lines.

More cautious—and yet at the same time an aggressive leader in communications, in electronic journalism: bold, fearless, daring. *Yes*—if he or she knows when to be which—when to avoid attacking windmills and when to be Prince Valiant or Queen Aleta; when to listen to clamorous voices and when to stand firm; when to offer the chin and when to duck; when—as previously stated—to anticipate the *consequences* of a decision or line of action.

To conclude: the chapters in Part III are *situation statements.*

Essay, *yes:* personal bias: *yes:* advice from friends: *yes*. Reflecting on *Case Studies First Edition,* one broadcast educator confided that many of his students wished to find the "correct" answers in the back of the book, or at least in the hands of the instructor.

I could only answer that *there are no correct answers*—at least in comparison to a text in math or geology. The subject is too contemporary, subject to ever-changing rulings, unscientific to withstand the scrutiny of multiplying to infinity or digging below the Pre-Cambrian shield. Superficial readings in the broadcast trade papers tell us that success is not enough—if the never-ending game of musical chairs played in network executive suites is a reliable barometer.

These, then, are a series of exercises in *reasoning out* what may be the best way to go, be that best way modified by profit-and-loss charts, community relations, guidelines of regulatory agencies, industry trends, advice from industry trade associations, or whatever. To repeat: *to attempt to induce the ability to anticipate the consequences of a decision or line of action.*

ACKNOWLEDGEMENTS

To what is now called *ConRail,* operators of the New Haven Division of the suburban railroad I ride weekdays, whose erratic operation has permitted me valuable hours of conversation with some of the finest brains in the communications field . . .

And to R. Marshall Stross and his staff—my everyday colleagues—who share with me their opinions and information in a way I never knew among the long knives of commercial broadcasting . . .

For kind words and encouragement: Bob Boulware of the International Radio and Television Society; Les Brown of the New York *Times;* Ken Mills of Katz Television; Ted Zydel of Young and Rubicam . . .

Who ever says anything nice about his publisher? To Russell Neale of Hastings House, for nodding, smiling, saying "go ahead" . . .

And as ever to a patient family, an exactingly-demanding proof-reading team of wife and daughter, the most thanks of all.

Larchmont, N.Y. January 1978

SUGGESTED READINGS

The suggested readings below, cued to the various chapters—in some cases specific by chapter, and in others general—assume several basic readings: Professional periodicals, e.g., the *Television Quarterly* and the *Journal of Broadcasting, Broadcasting* magazine, *Television/Radio Age, Variety, Media Decisions, Advertising Age,* and other news-and-feature publications devoting major space to commercial broadcast matters.

Since I have no thrust in advancing these papers in any grove, academe or not, the references cited are minimal: only those known to the writer are listed. It is assumed that the serious communications student has access to and familiarity with the major works of Eric Barnouw, the many effluvial outpourings of Marshall McLuhan, and the scores of references that cross themselves in the back of every major text. Gutenberg in his 15th century lifetime never had it so good as the paper salesman in the 20th!

(1) Bluem, William A. *Religious Television Programs: A Study of Relevance.* New York: Hastings House, 1969.
(2) Brown, Lester (ed.) *Encyclopedia of Television.* New York: Quadrangle/New York Times Book Co., 1977.
(3) Coleman, Howard W. (ed.) *Color Television: The Business of Colorcasting.* New York: Hastings House, 1968.
(4) de Sola Pool, Ithiel, and Wilbur Schramm, etc. *Handbook of Communications.* Chicago: Rand McNally College Publishing Co., 1973.

(5) Ellens, J. Harold. *Models of Religious Broadcasting*. Grand Rapids, Mich.: Eerdmans Publishing, 1974.

(6) Emery, Walter. *Broadcasting and Government: Responsibilities and Regulations*. East Lansing, Mich.: Michigan State University Press, 1971.

(7) Friendly, Fred W. *The Good Guys, the Bad Guys, and the First Amendment: Free Speech vs. Fairness in Broadcasting*. New York: Random House, 1976.

(8) Jordan, Lewis (ed.) *The New York Times Manual of Style and Usage*. New York: Quadrangle/The New York Times Book Company, 1976.

(9) Lichty, Lawrence W. and Malachi C. Topping. *American Broadcasting: A Source Book on the History of Radio and Television*. New York: Hastings House, 1975.

(10) Melody, William. *Children's Television: The Economics of Exploitation*. New Haven, Conn.: Yale University Press, 1973.

(11) Newman, Edwin. *Strictly Speaking*. Indianapolis, Ind.: Bobbs-Merrill, 1974.

(12) Quaal, Ward L. and James A. Brown. *Broadcast Management: Radio + Television,* 2nd Edition. New York: Hastings House, 1976.

(13) Rivers, William L. *The Mass Media*. New York: Harper & Row, 1975.

(14) Roe, Yale (ed.) *Television Station Management*. New York: Hastings House, 1964.

(15) Small, William. *To Kill A Messenger: Television News and the Real World*. New York: Hastings House, 1970.

(16) Stanley, Robert H. (ed.) *The Broadcast Industry: An Examination of Major Issues*. New York: Hastings House, 1975.

(17) Stanley, Robert H. and Charles Steinberg. *The Media Environment*. New York: Hastings House, 1976.

(18) Steinberg, Charles S. *The Creation of Consent*. New York: Hastings House, 1975.

(19) Zuckman, Harvey L. and Martin J. Gaynes. *Mass Communications Law in a Nutshell*. St. Paul, Minn.: West Publishing, 1977.

A WRITER'S OPINION . . .

To approach broadcasting as a career, it is this writer's opinion that the student should have a comprehension of significant elements of communication from hieroglyphics to the Gutenberg moveable-type press to the satellite; from the Ten Commandments, the Magna Carta, Luther's 95 Theses to Thomas Paine's *Common Sense* and Lincoln's Gettysberg Address; from the 1906 broadcast from Brant Rock, Mass., to the conversation between the President of the United States and the commander of the first lunar landing craft . . . and to an afternoon of direct telephone conversations between another President and his constituency.

In that context the serious student can bring to each of the case studies a fresh approach, a challenge, an alternative.

Without that background and that approach, *more of the same* promises to be the *name of the game.*

PART I

Case Study Problems

1

TELEVISION VIOLENCE

... violence presented on the media should be condemned only when it is presented for its own sake, when it exploits its audience and when its consequences are morally and socially indefensible. In that last analysis, the media cannot pretend that violence does not exist. Those who would prefer to avoid exposure to media portrayal of violence have the option to turn off the set or close the book.

Robert H. Stanley and Charles S. Steinberg in *The Media Environment*.

What was very likely the first investigation into the influence of TV violence on children, at least in the form of an inquiry by a governmental body, was held in Chicago in late 1952.

The hearings were inspired by a column by *Daily News* writer Jack Mabley, who reported that his wife and a group of suburban Glenview neighbors had made a pact to sit home on a given Saturday morning, view with their children the video fare offered, and log the acts of violence observed.

Mabley reported the gross figure of what these eight or nine ladies had ticked off, without much editorial comment. *Something over 200;* it was the same figure that he offered—Lincolnesque style, from the back of an envelope—at the subsequent hearing.

A West Side alderman, significantly one up for re-election, convened the hearings in Chicago's City Hall council chambers. After the submission of the Mabley envelope, which proved to be a gross of what all the ladies had viewed more or less simultaneously, there was a moment of letdown. Then the Windy City's police commissioner was called for his opinion, and he had a firm statement intoned with a leftover Irish brogue: "Sure and I told my son and daughter-in-law not to be letting my grandchildren watch that awful filth!"

Subsequent questioning showed that the grandchildren were three months and 19 months, and that line of attack was dropped.

The intellectual alderman from the city's University of Chicago section then offered a comment: "If 8.5 mothers, viewing simultaneously, reported about 200 acts of violence, I find this might *net* about 23.5 actual acts of violence on Chicago television, in the period from 7:30 a.m. to 1:00 p.m. on a Saturday morning. And since most of these programs are cartoons—Bugs Bunny and Crusader Rabbit and the like—I must assume that these acts of violence are the kinds of excesses we have laughed at ever since the Mickey Mouse silents. Does anyone have any contrary information?"

No one did. The intellectual alderman remembered another engagement, and excused himself. Several others followed. There was a suggestion that there was no longer a quorum present. The convening chairman rumbled out, muttering that "we sure must have a problem here."

He repeated his statement in the elevator, and O'Malley, the operator, was quick to agree: "Sure and yez do, sir. Like I keeps sayin' to me neighbors, if only folks would keep their kids in off the streets an' watchin' the telly, there wouldn't be all this joovee-nile deelinquence!"

The elevator reached the first floor, and the chairman got off, still looking puzzled. "Just keep 'em home," O'Malley called, "watchin' the fights an' the hockey an' the ball games, an' our cops'll have a lot less to do!"

> "His first polysyllable utterance was 'Bradybunch.' He learned to spell Sugar Snacks before his own name. He has seen Monte Carlo, witnessed a cocaine bust in Harlem and already has full-color fantasies involving Farrah Fawcett-

Majors. Recently, he tried to karate-chop his younger sister after she broke his Six Million Dollar Man transport station. (She retaliated by bashing him with her Cher doll.) His nursery-school teacher reports that he is passive, noncreative, unresponsive to instruction, bored during play periods, and possessed of an almost nonexistent attention span —in short, very much like his classmates. Next fall, he will officially reach the age of reason and begin his formal education. His parents are beginning to discuss their apprehensions—when they are not too busy watching television."

> . . . from the cover story, *What TV Does to Kids—Newsweek,* February 21, 1977

Somber words from a news arbiter about a four-year-old. In other pages of that same *Newsweek* issue, there were such offerings as these: *Thoughts of Brother Billy* (On Religion)—"Bunch of damned hypocrites down there at that Baptist Church. The only time I go is when one of the kids is baptized.". . . from another feature, *Pulling the Big Switch:* "Goddam it, I'm telling you the truth . . . A hell of a good thing if reporters knew . . ." In pages 60–61 the magazine showed as top-flight an array of ladies in underthings as *Playboy* ever did in its relative age of innocence before the competition introduced absolute nudity as a standard. Also, a giggly review of the movie, *Fun with Dick and Jane,* wherein the protagonists turn to armed robbery as a solution when they run out of money. And win.

The same issue carried eight advertisements for cigarettes, four for hard liquors—and, incredible if you believe editorial content, two pages of ads for television sets!

The easy defense for *Newsweek* is to say that the four-year-old, who can only spell Sugar Snacks (not an advertiser) is not fair game for its own content. But what about the 12-year-old, who is and who most surely has access to the family copy? *Taylor, the premium sherry . . . Chivas Regal . . . Fun and Games with Dick and Jane . . . Now* and *Salem* and *Parliament . . .* Billy Carter describing his Baptist friends as a "damned bunch of hypocrites."

Which, in the 12-year-old mind, was fact, or opinion, or "just" advertising?

. . .

To the subject, does anyone speak for the broadcaster?

H. M. Turner, chief executive of MacLaren Advertising, Canada's largest advertising agency, said this (*Advertising Age,* May 9, 1977): "It fascinates me that the attacks are on the world of fantasy, not real life. Is this because we can't face the shock of real violence? It seems to me that we are all in constant and serious danger of losing our sense of context."

The *AA* article was headed "TV violence wrong target for print," and said that "The print media, feeling threatened by television, have deliberately misrepresented the issues of violence on television."

"Some portrayals of violence are very good and important for people to see on television, and good for children to see," Turner quoted criminologist Melvin Miller as saying. A violent police show, such as *Kojak,* is no more than "a fairy tale for the middle-aged adult frustrated by his helplessness and lonely for the dreams of an adulthood full of power and heroism . . . they are always on the side of God and good government, they prove that institutional values are safe ones, and they prove that outcasts always lose."

What does Webster's say about violence?

". . . broadly, exertion of any physical force considered with reference to another than the agent, as in warfare, or in effecting an entrance into a house in burglary. Sometimes, in law, the overcoming or prevention of resistance by violence or threat of violence is held to be constructive violence."

The ABC Network's stated working definition of *violence* is: "Force or compelling threat of force resulting in harm to life. Violent force may also be exerted against valued objects. Violence involves harmful or antisocial consequences."

CBS defined violence: "The use of physical force against persons or animals, or the articulated, expressed threat of physical force to compel particular behavior on the part of a person."

The American Association of Advertising Agencies toe-danced around the issue with the statement: "We believe that, since advertising supports TV, it is obligatory for agencies—as a service to their clients—to restudy advertising commitments to programs which feature violence. Some advertisers may feel that it is worth paying a higher price to reach an audience through different programs."

ABC-TV president, James Duffy, speaking before the 1977 4A meeting, emphasized that the network will not let the violence issue be misused by taking human conflict out of TV drama and leaving in only the bland and the boring. "There are two ominous trends to be found in the persistence of criticism over an issue which, to any rational or reasonable person, has ended. One is censorship and the other is what the psychologists call projection—the projecting of blame for a problem that is too difficult to handle —onto some handy scapegoat."

How Did It All Come About?

On the premise that few out of a hundred have ever read the report of the U.S. Surgeon General on *Television Violence,* here is an abridged version of what *Variety* reported from Washington on March 21, 1972: "A strong and unequivocal statement by the U.S. Surgeon General that 'television violence, indeed, does have an adverse effect on certain members of our society' today seemed almost certain to increase pressure on the networks to restrict violence in entertainment programming.

"Senate communications subcommittee chairman John O. Pastore (D.RI) asked for a straightforward interpretation of the academic findings of the Surgeon General's panel on violence that he initiated two years ago, and Dr. Jesse Steinfeld gave it to him. Steinfeld said that 'my professional response today is that the broadcasters should be put on notice.

"Scientists will never unanimously agree on 'a succinct statement of causality,' Steinfeld opined. 'But there comes a time when the data are sufficient to justify action—that time has come.'. . .

"Steinfeld cautioned against making 'television the whipping boy for all of society's ills,' but he also said no action against TV violence is a form of action: 'it is an acquiescense in the continuation of the present level of televised violence entering American homes.' "

How Do You Face What Issue?

In the April 11, 1977 *Broadcasting,* the report is headed: *United Church takes on mission against sex and violence on TV.* In capsule form, the story reports a "Pronouncement on the Use of Gratuitous Violence and the Exploitation of Sex on Television"; says that it "denounces television for its pathological preoccupation with violence and sex, and calls on all elements of the church to interest themselves in the governmental and private decisions that shape governing, to resist the use of gratuitous violence and the exploitation of sex in programming, and 'to demand programs that portray human life realistically and honestly in all of its facets, including conflict and sex.' "

. . .

As reported in *Advertising Age* (May 16, 1977), "the issue of TV violence gained momentum and has continued to grow as such companies as General Foods, Best Foods, Gillette, Samsonite, Sears, Revlon, Pillsbury, Eastman Kodak, Hallmark, Goodyear, Ralston Purina, Kimberly-Clark, Helene Curtis Industries and Greyhound Corp. record their objections."

The National Citizens Committee for Broadcasting in 1976 began issuing a "violence rating" list that named advertisers sponsoring violent programming. The American Medical Association supported the NCCB's work with a grant. The National Congress of Parents and Teachers also has been involved in efforts to check TV violence, believing that the screening of murders, fights, rapes, muggings, robberies, beatings and kidnappings could affect the attitudes of children.

In May 1977 the national P-TA announced a "First Action Plan," to run from July to the end of the year. It involved a "massive letter-writing campaign" from the group's 6.5 million members. With no substantial response by January 1978, P-TA officers said they would boycott advertisers and programs and institute civil suits to prevent station license renewal.

Rebuttal from the Television Information Office of the National Association of Broadcasters: the Roper research organization reported that only 39 per cent of Americans believe that "violent action in television entertainment programs" is a major cause of children's aggressive and hostile behavior. From Roper: 79 per cent of respondents blamed lack of home discipline for poor child behavior; 45 per cent listed "unhappy or broken homes" and 43 per cent cited "too much free time and not enough to do."

From another arena, a quote from the 1977 annual report of Westinghouse to its stockholders: "Timothy Smith of New York City, the director of the Interfaith Center on Corporate Responsibility, asked if Westinghouse or Group W has established any policy on the question of violence on television. Donald H. McGannon, chairman of Group W, said that he believes there is too much violence on television, and that Group W has petitioned the FCC to require the networks to give adequate time for local stations to preview programs. That petition is still pending."

Now McGannon or one of his coterie forgot something: in truth that "petition" was written into the FCC regulations a long time ago; maybe conveniently forgotten, but still there. *Right to reject programs.* "No license shall be granted to a television station having any contract, arrangement or understanding, express or implied, with a network organization which, with respect to programs offered or already contracted for pursuant to an affiliation contract, prevents or hinders the station from (1) rejecting or refusing network programs which the station reasonably believes to be unsuitable or contrary to the public interest, or (2) substituting a program which in the station's opinion is of greater local or national interest."

Possibly Mr. McGannon was being a bit defensive. With the flexibility of videotape at both the sending and receiving ends of the network systems, the pre-screening of network programs must be considered an almost-mechanical function—subject to the judgmental capabilities of the person at the receiving end of the pre-screening video feed.

And that person may well be the most sensitive link the station has with its public!

That earlier-referred-to *Advertising Age* issue of May 16, 1977, also carried a page 1 story headed "TV violence issue burning itself out," stating the General Foods' director of media services, Archa O. Knowlton, "came to his first Congressional hearing primed with figures showing that General Foods saw 'marked improvement' in the recently-announced 1977–1978 network schedule (re TV violence)."

But nobody on the Senate communications subcommittee asked him the question. And the May 23, 1977 *Broadcasting* reported: "P-TA schools members in pressure tactics." The story said that the national P-TA task force had begun "training troops for its declared war on TV violence."

"New study downplays TV effect on young" was the lead in a June 6, 1977 article in *Broadcasting*. From a two-year study of 341 Marion, Ill., families with fourth, fifth and sixth grade children, the reporting research team concluded that TV does affect children already prone to violence—some 20 per cent of all child viewers—but said it is difficult to identify the children that fit in that category.

Southern Illinois University professors Charles Klasek and Nancy Quisenberry observed that they respect organizations such as the P-TA for attempting to clean up television, but they think these groups exaggerate the negative influence of the medium on the young.

"There just hasn't been enough research done to indicate television has the profound effect on children that many people and groups are claiming it has," Klasek said.

The SIU research team offered these additional conclusions:

- TV viewing does not hurt school achievement appreciably. They said it does not seem to matter how much TV a child watches, unless he or she is viewing late at night. Children who watch after 10 p.m. apparently do show lower achievement levels.
- Many children do watch TV in the late-night and early morning hours, making the family viewing hour pointless.
- The criticism that TV interferes with religious beliefs appears unfounded.

The research team also said that parents are more sensitive to what their children watch than some groups think.

What Next?

Broadcasting on May 23, 1977 editorialized that ". . . It is obvious that television violence is losing its appeal as a cause. That leaves those whose livelihoods depend on causes to look for something else to criticize. A likely target is television profits, and broadcasters had better be prepared."

That same week *Advertising Age* headed a story from Detroit: "Sex next to go from TV screen," quoting Campbell-Ewald agency media director Tom Glynn. He said that TV violence has been "garroted, stomped, mangled and killed. Violence has passed away.

"The number of situation comedies will be staggering," Glynn continued. "Next to go will be sex and permissiveness, as pressure groups emerge . . . the genius of creativity will yield to large committees brought back to dull things up. Someone with a bright, pertinent idea will be subjected to a committee."

THE CASE STUDY PROBLEM: You are the station manager, TV market between the 25th and 50th, are a network affiliate, have two network competitors plus one independent station in your area, and two cable systems serving distant parts of your signal area.

The subject of TV violence will come up again and again. *As,* we read, will *sex* and *permissiveness*—which will need new definitions. *From whence cometh?* A sincere local group with a concern, or a group stimulated by a national civic or religious organization? Does the attack make sense, or is it simply part of a coordinated activity?

If that attack is from a sincere local group, *you* may well be at fault. What's wrong with your local public service programming?

But if it's stimulated from outside, are you prepared? *And how you prepare yourself is the challenge of this case study.*

SUGGESTED READINGS

(4) deSola Pool and Schramm — see references under "violence."
(5) Ellens — see "Morality in Media."
(10) Melody — general background under the topic.
(12) Quaal and Brown — see references to "Violence on TV."
(16) Stanley — see references under "Children's programming."
(17) Stanley and Steinberg — see various legal interpretations under "Mass Communications and the Supreme Court."

2

STATION REVENUE AND THE STATION MANAGER

. . . I think we'll continue to sell advertising but we've got to do a better job. We can't sit there and wait for the phone to ring. We've got to get out and develop new markets. We (at WAGA-TV) have a sales development team that doesn't do anything but develop sales. This is a full-time job. Once they've developed a sale, it's turned over to the sales department and then they go on to something else. I'm optimistic over the long-range. I think we'll be able to survive and to continue to make a profit.

> Terry McGuirk, WAGA-TV Atlanta, in
> *The Broadcast Industry: An Examination
> of Major Issues* (16)

THE BACKGROUND

Joe Butterfield sits in a solid position as station manager of a substantial TV station in a medium market—255,000 TV households; two competitors; each of the three stations the fulltime affiliate of one of three major networks.

Joe reports to Charles Simon, vice president and general manager. Simon is a minority stockholder, a member of the board of directors of the group owning the station, as well as a radio station, a publishing firm and other properties. Due to a wide spread of interests on Simon's part, Joe has the challenge of full operating control of the station—a situation not always present in broadcasting.

Historically, the station came into existence in early 1953, just following the FCC "freeze" of TV channel licensing; has had a steady growth in its market since that time; along with its two competitors has enjoyed increased income as TV household set counts moved up, and as rate cards moved up with them, as more of the advertisers' dollars have been diverted to television advertising.

The Problem

For many years the TV station has been the outstanding profit-maker among the properties controlled by the investment group. However, the sharp climb in TV households tapered off as TV reached a near-saturation point; rate card increases tapered off as well—and so did net profits.

At the same time labor costs continued high . . . spiraling cost of living and greater stability of employees demanded steady salary increases, increased benefits . . . the cost of station operation curved upward at a sharper rate than profits.

The board of directors was well aware of the nature of the situation, and scaled budgets accordingly. They retained a broadcast consultant as well as a Washington law firm; knew that their situation was far from unique, and that they were in at least as favorable a position as other stations with the same network affiliation in comparable markets. But at the same time they looked for ways both to control costs and to increase revenue.

Butterfield was asked to prepare for an all-day, full scale meeting with Simon and the corporate controller, R. J. Clawson, following the annual board meeting in February. Indicated in advance were two major agenda points: (1) economies in operation, and (2) increased revenue potential.

As a first step in preparing for the meeting, Butterfield detailed the present situation. In most segments of the broadcast day revenues were fairly well fixed, as influenced by the TV set saturation of the market, with an expansion rate closely tied to the national rate of population and household growth and reasonably anticipated at one or two per cent per year.

Station Revenue and the Station Manager

Compensation from the network (for carrying programs) was set from an elaborate formula, adjusted year-by-year.

Billings from national and regional advertisers in local spots were pretty well scaled by competitive pricing, by measurable audience, and guided by the station's national sales representative. While Butterfield as a good manager always pressed his reps for "another 10%," he was fair with them and his employer in rating them as doing a good job in delivering national business: "In most months of the year they bring in more than one-third of the total national spot business in this three-station market."

Locally the station logged a well-rounded roster of clients: financial institutions, car dealer associations and dealers, beer and soft drink bottlers, appliance and home furnishings retailers and the rest. Rates here, as with network compensation and national spot billings, were pretty well solidified by market saturation and competitive pricing.

The cost of station operation, of *doing business,* continued to climb, however—at a rate exceeding that of sales revenue. Talent and labor costs were as competitive as other aspects of the three-station economy, and contract prices for the use of program materials—primarily feature films and syndicated programs—continued to rise in anticipation of the needs of the highest bidder.

As the station operation matured, salaries and benefits multiplied. The TV station management and staff had been brought into the corporate fringe benefits plans in the late 1950's; insurance and pension reserves and profit sharing became a heavier overhead load as a higher percentage of 10-, 15- and soon-to-be 20-year employees dominated the payroll.

In all overall review of these points, Butterfield's best estimate was that of a continuing-profit operation, but on a descending scale: one that could, under present methods of operation, deliver predictable-but-modest net profits for a number of years ahead— but that did *not* promise to reverse the trend of the past two or more years and *increase* that profit ratio.

Seeking a Solution

Butterfield presented the problem to his staff: national sales manager Bob Frank; local sales manager Wally Olsen; program manager Mort Samuels; chief engineer Bill England. In both his memo on the subject (outlining his preliminary survey) and in the following meeting, he included the station business manager, Nate Archer, and the promotion manager, Hal Barton.

At that meeting, he staked out ground rules for procedure: The subject under discussion is *increased profitability,* and it is to be explored in two ways—*economy in operation* and *higher revenues.*

"This is off the record, and informal," he continued, "but most serious in attempting to reach a decision that will offer a promise of solving the problem. Who's first?"

Samuels, the program manager, spoke: "In this central time zone, we really carry the late night network show an hour ahead of the East, and sign off an hour earlier than stations in most eastern markets. I think we could add a one-hour strip film show, or even two 30-minute shows, and keep some late-night audience."

"Cost you overtime," the chief engineer rumbled.

"But," Butterfield asked the sales managers, "could it be sold?"

Bob Frank hedged his reply: *"If* it showed up with some fair rating points, we could maybe bring in a couple of spots on Fridays and Saturdays—maybe even Thursdays—but forget about the early part of the week!"

Local sales manager Olsen was cautious: "We might get some of the all-night fast-food outfits interested, or a discount clothing chain—but we'd be competing with all-night radio and it would have to be at a very reasonable price."

The promotion manager entered a program note: "Some really wild programming, like the *Cisco Kid* as it's dubbed for foreign markets, or silent movies with funny comment—but we'd have to spend some extra money on promotion."

Butterfield noted Point One: the possibility of extending the broadcast day, in anticipation of holding audience and offering more availabilities for spot announcements or sponsorship.

Olsen was next: "I know about the FCC and licenses and everything, but I think we carry an awful lot of sustaining programs from the network. Our competitor over here knocks out that religious show from New York at noon on Sunday, and has a movie sponsored by Swift Real Estate, and at five o'clock they carry that Star Trek series instead of the network interview show from Washington. If we did something like that I know we could get some local business."

Frank shook his head: "No national business for Sunday daytime."

Butterfield noted Point Two: the possibility of pre-empting some network sustaining shows, particularly on Sundays, to accommodate potential local advertising. He also noted the need to check policy with the law firm in Washington, and to re-check the actions of his competitors.

Bill England, chief engineer, spoke: "We log a tremendous amount of man hours taping commercials for local clients. I know this is a necessary service, but I think we should draw up some new ground rules. These guys come in without any real plan, only an outline of a script, and goof around for as long as we'll let 'em, trying new shots and arty ideas. This costs money—real money. How about some limits, and a realistic scale of charges?"

Defending his local clients, Olsen replied heatedly: "These guys don't have any other place to go, except to our competition! We've got to give them service when they buy time!"

"That's true, Wally," England responded, "but *they* don't run the service end of their businesses at a loss, and *we* can't afford to either. Electronic equipment has a predictable life span, and electricity costs money, and the biggest cost of all is overtime technical manpower."

Butterfield wrote Point Three: a close examination of studio and overall production use by clients, with the possibility of setting firmer rates and ground rules for commercial production.

Bob Frank spoke forcefully: "We are locked in by hours of network programming that are spelled out for us. In most of the prime time spots, and in the daytime soap operas and the rest of the network daytime schedule, we can sell national spot clients without too much trouble.

"But we are losing potential additional income at night, in our 10-to-10:30 news-weather-sports strip. Seven nights a week we have a parade of oldtime local sponsors. We get to sell some spots in-between the shows, but the programs themselves are all locked up by one or two, maybe even three sponsors, on a 52-week basis. And that's on a local rate, 52-week discount basis, I want to add!"

"Yeah," Olsen interrupted, "but they don't go in and out with fancy agency-conceived 'flights'—they *are* there every week."

"I'm willing to take my chances," Frank continued. "In off-season time some local guy can always be brought in anyway, and at a higher and shorter rate. We could get extra prime time revenue if we tossed these guys out and made the programs available only for one-minute spot announcements or whatever. Joe, I say we should clean everybody out between 10 and 10:30, and make the whole period open to spot announcements!"

Olsen was adamant: "Some of these local people have been with us for better than five years, and First National Bank has been on the Sunday news since it went on the air. Toss 'em out, and you're in for a lot of grief in town!"

Samuels sighed: "Look, we *say* that we have a news-weather-sports block where whatever is most important comes first. But we bow to the fact that these longtime sponsors want a specific identification with a personality."

"All that I'm saying," Frank went on, "is that I think we *do* have an opportunity—within our broadcast day and without adding hours or extra program or labor cost—to offer availabilities that will bring in more sales dollars."

"But don't forget," Nate Archer added, "that this national business has buried in the sales dollars the commission for the agency and the commission for the sales rep—much of this local business comes to us *direct*—no agency—and we produce the commercial materials as needed."

"And," Frank added, "we then have to employ writers and directors to do it—and we still have the commissions paid the local salesmen."

As POINT FOUR, Butterfield noted the suggestion of turning the already-profitable nighttime news-weather-sports strip over to spot participation only, rather than the largely proprietary interest sponsorship situation now present.

By prior talks, Butterfield dismissed change or reduction in the various seasonal promotion plans sketched out by Barton as a factor in long-range economy considerations: it was agreed that an aggressive promotion plan was required in any event, and that current activity was flexible enough to be shifted to place emphasis on most programming changes that might be made.

The meeting closed, Butterfield turned to an examination of

the major points brought out, as he would present them before his management:

POINT ONE: The possibility of extending the broadcast day, staying on the air an hour or more later than the present schedule and offering some form of programming to attract night owls. He listed program costs as minimal, some promotion costs to attract that specialized audience, labor costs as a major factor, income from national spot business as a weekend possibility, local business as marginal but with some potential.

POINT TWO: Pre-empting network programming at key times when the possibility of sales to local clients might make this profitable. Olsen had been pinpointing a few weekend periods when a non-sponsored or public service program might be blanked out; Butterfield looked at possibilities beyond this: in the area, Friday night was late shopping night, with virtually all retail outlets open until 10 p.m. and the suburban plazas and malls jammed with cars. He noted: what about a two-hour "shoppers' special" in the middle of Friday afternoon, and an hour of features on the news-weather-sports side from 6 to 7 p.m., with 60-second spots open to local advertising?

POINT THREE: England had brought to a head a long-simmering point of debate—how far do you go, and how much do you bend, in aiding local advertisers and agencies in the production of commercial materials? At a modest $10 a minute for a live studio with full staff, how many minutes can you give? The other stations must be in the same bind; possibly this is the time to set a firm schedule of rates for use of studio time.

POINT FOUR: A major re-alignment of commercial practices in the well-rated 10–10:30 p.m. program strip. With the reasonable guarantee of a good lead-in audience from the network at 10 p.m., this has the promise of being a continuing top property. To toss out the existing local clients was a risk of a loss in good will as well as revenue; the possibility of bringing in a solid list of national spot clients indeed offered at least a 10% increase in revenue for the time period. Semi-annual price increases would be more normal and expected in this national spot advertising frame of reference.

Other areas? The staff was solid, paid but not overpaid for their efforts—there was little but inefficiency and lowered morale to be gained by a staff reduction.

What *could* be achieved had to be done within the framework of the four segmented areas outlined by his department heads.

THE CASE STUDY PROBLEM: As Joe Butterfield, develop a plan of minimum 12-month scope, preferably 24 months, to meet the management goal of *increased profitability* through *economy in operation* and *higher revenues*.

SUGGESTED READINGS

(12) Quaal and Brown — chapter 5 ("Costs of local programming").
(14) Roe — chapter 1 ("The business of broadcasting").
(16) Stanley — see "Program content; or, what are we going to do to fill the time between commercials?"

3

THE RADIO AUDIENCE: WHERE IS IT, HOW DO WE ACQUIRE MORE?

"Leading radio stations, total day, metro area," were reported in the February 14, 1977 issue of *Television/Radio Age,* based on data from October/November Arbitron reports; markets ranked by total revenues according to FCC 1975 information by metro markets PROGRAM CODES. (The total report, which also offers data on standings in various dayparts, all in markets one-through-75, may be found in that periodical, updated at least annually.)

What guidelines may be found to most successful program formats? That's the key question to what may be deduced, with a lot of painstaking research, from these data.

In terms of total day share-of-audience, *rock* stations scored number one in the first and ninth markets; *all-news* was first in the fourth and sixth markets, third in the first, third and seventh markets (also fourth in the first market); *talk* was first in the number two market and second in the number one and number four markets.

But note that *various,* meaning a mixed bag, scored number one in markets three, eight and ten, second in markets seven and eight.

In the following case study, the Marsh Report attempts to bring some resolution to a serious programming problem. It must be remembered that, due to the numbers of radio signals available in these markets, the relative standings are often from two points down to a decimal point apart. Some do better: in only one instance—and here we name names—WCCO Minneapolis shows a 30.8 share over the 8.3 of its nearest rival! This has been the case for many years; the program expert who finds the secret will be dubbed *Sir Gawain* by the Radio Advertising Bureau!

THE BACKGROUND

When PLB Corporation purchased its paired radio and TV properties in Everytown, it became the owner of two decidedly different broadcast outlets: 1. A successful TV station, with a solid network affiliation and a fair share of the viewing audience; 2. A fumbling-along-the-middle-of-the-road radio station, with audiences that in the most optimistic rating report rarely achieved more than 10% of the total listening public.

Mack Grainger, PLB group vice president, summed up the owner's point of view for a meeting of WAAA-Radio executives: "We are here to do a successful long-range job. In TV our problems are relatively small—they are not *your* problems, and I promise you that radio will not be considered a minor promotion vehicle for TV.

"WAAA-Radio came on the air here in the mid-20's, and was a pioneer station and a major voice in the market before TV. As in many other situations, management lost interest when the video tube began to glow brighter and brighter in the 1950's. A parade of program managers and disc jockeys did so many things in the past 10 years that I doubt whether there is an original listener left.

"Just a year ago, a 'program doctor' from the sales rep firm turned it into a hard-rock station—even though there were, and are, two stations of that type in Everytown.

"The net result was to alienate every older listener, and *not* to draw many new ones away from the two established rockers. But it took six months to discover this. Since then—and with a complete staff turnover—WAAA has been stumbling along a path that doesn't seem to lead anywhere."

THE PROBLEM

"We have a very simple problem, and a large challenge," Grainger continued. "PLB wants this to be a good station, a solid station, a significant voice in the community. We have no set formulas for this—in four different markets, we have four different types of stations, and the only common denominator is that they each have a recognizable voice in the market.

"I've asked the home office to lend you Hank Marsh, for the specific purpose of surveying this situation and coming up with recommendations for a new WAAA voice. Note that I *didn't* say 're-program'—I said 'make recommendations.' I really mean a long-range job. Hank is not a quickie program doctor, and you are not pressed by time in that sense.

"*You* people are going to have to do the actual programming and selling and operating, and live with it. What Hank comes up with will be spelled out in detail. Where we go from there will be what you decide. After whatever period of time it takes, Hank will deliver a report; we will all go over it in detail, and press to come up with a pattern for the future that will put WAAA in a solid position in the market."

THE MARSH REPORT

1. *The Competition*

In this market of 1.2 million population there are 10 AM radio stations regularly reportable in the audience surveys; also one FM station—but with a program format so specialized that we need not consider it for the purpose at hand.

The remaining six AM and two FM stations collectively represent less than 5% of the audience.

The two top stations, *A* and *B,* both are 50 kw clear channel stations; as such they offer varied programming to reach beyond the metropolitan area. *A* is more traditional; *B* has a slightly more youthful sound in its voices and music, but basically is in that same regional service category.

2. *The 'Real' Competition*

We face four other stations in the fight for a share of the local audience. *C* is a 50 kw directional signal hard-rock station; *D* at 5 kw has a similar content, but with less of *C*'s "hey kids" and more of a "Hello, youth of all ages" appeal. Between them, they certainly offer at least enough of that kind of programming for Everytown.

The remaining competitors, including us, are all at the 5 kw, full-time service level, entirely adequate for reaching our metropolitan market. Station *E* defies strict categorization: it offers musical periods of nostalgia and "Americana," but at other hours has a talk program followed by musical comedy favorites of past years.

Station *F* has very little music; makes sounds like a combination of a "talk" station and an all-news format. Whatever they are doing seems subject to change, including syndicated shows and remotes from retail locations.

We—WAAA—aren't doing anything *bad;* Mack's summation might in turn be summarized with one word—*lackluster*. To lay further burden on an already-overworked word, we don't have any *image*. I don't mean to suggest that this in itself is a major criticism: the dominant station *A* doesn't operate in any easily-definable category. It has personalities and news and jazz and concerts and farm hours—the image is in the minds of the large numbers of different audiences it commands at different times of the broadcast day. But that's an extremely expensive way to go, and can be justified only with the kind of income to be drawn from a major operation.

3. *Where Do We Go?*

Let's run through the list of formats present in radio today—each has been successful in many markets; none is present in absolute practice here in Everytown today.

  a. *The All-News Station*—This is a well-established formula; has achieved great success in many major markets. It turns up a fresh re-hash of news headlines every 15 or 20 minutes in peak listening hours; shoots in quick weather and traffic and time information; possibly enhances its fare with a shotgun pattern of special taped features in off hours.

  The concept was developed to establish an image of a place where you could get everything you needed in a brief time period.

  On the negative side, it demands a large staff—possibly 40 or more readers, writers and editors to go on a

mands a music director of wide classical background, and well-educated writers, announcers and newsmen.

e. *The Country-Western Station*—In one sense, this is about as far removed from the classical pattern above as you could get—the first impression would be that we were shooting for a 100% *different* audience in *d.* above as compared to *e.* here. But today's country-western has shed its red flannel shirts and washdresses, hay-chewing and pigtails. The music goes beyond the three chords of the hillbilly's guitar, and the lyrics cover subjects more varied than just leaving that old Red River Valley. The instrumental backings are more often than not done by reeds and violins and brass sections, and the names are not all Fud and Minnie.

I mean this in its most favorable context when I say that country-western is a likeable and inoffensive format, with a lot of tuneful appeal for people who just might attend the symphony and the legitimate shows in other hours.

To Sum Up:

This is a far from complete list of radio program possibilities, but it's useful here in that it describes formats *not* present at the moment in your area of competition.

Two of the PLB AM stations are successful with a good music format; another is dominant with the all-talk operation. By way of contrast, we have one FM station doing a severe classical job, and another with a kind of "Americana" format only one step removed from straight country-western.

As I see it, you have a number of ways to go. Any one of these will, with proper promotion, give you an image of being a definable and identifiable voice; any one will also provide an effective vehicle for commercial messages for your clients; and any one will be an understandable commodity to be sold by your national sales reps.

The choice you make, or whatever combination of formats you devise, will have to be one that is most comfortable in terms of programming, promoting and selling.

round-the-clock basis, as compared to the 15 people employed here.

b. *The "Pure" Good Music Station*—This has had such labels as "gaslight music" and "the sound of beautiful music" and "wall-to-wall music." It minimizes the role of the disc jockey to that of an anonymous voice, uses quick musical passages on tape to bridge from one record to another, "clusters" commercials in groups while claiming uninterrupted musical segments of 10 or 11 minutes. News as such is offered briefly on the hour, and little short of a holocaust is reason to break the pre-recorded format.

It is initially expensive to establish and to promote; later very economical; has a success record in many medium-to-large markets.

c. *The All-Talk Station*—This balances fairly lengthy news and special events programs with non-musical "talk" shows: the cult of the personality is all-important. It depends in large measure on the loneliness of listeners, and their need to respond to what they hear. The personality may work alone, taking phone calls and in turn listening or responding; or he may have guest "experts" sit with him as an added inducement to public response. The technology of fast tape-delay conversation from the callers has reduced the dangers of crackpots and libel; however, the personality must be quick with his responses and decisions. This, as with the all-news format, is expensive: you can't give smart pills to ex-disc jockeys, and air personalities capable of giving this kind of program a successful aur can command top salaries. The consideration has to be made in light of the success of the format in many market

d. *The Classical Station*—This is on one hand a terribly limited format; on the other, the continued success of WQX in New York must be taken into account. In this mark of 1.2 million people, with its own symphony orchestr major universities, art centers, little theaters and other c tural activities, this is a format that must be consider Voices are of course anonymous; news is offered in a lo keyed, non-tabloid sort of way, and special programs geared to a fairly well-defined audience stratum.

It is not as cheap a format as it might seem: it

The Radio Audience

The Question: Which Way to Go?

Grainger underscored a problem, and in a very real sense issued a challenge.

Marsh first of all summed up the current radio market situation in detail; secondly indicated a realistic view of the competitive situation; thirdly offered five possible ways to go.

There are six WAAA-Radio executives whose roles must be analyzed in the decision-making process:

BURNS, the station manager, who will bear the ultimate responsibility.

SWANSON, the national sales manager, who must concern himself with acceptance of the new format by advertising agencies involved with national spot advertising.

FRANK, the local sales manager, with a major interest in a type of programming that will be attractive to local clients (who actually tune in and listen to the showcasing of their own advertising).

BAINS, the program manager, who will have overall control and day-by-day responsibility for the station's product.

AIELLO, the operations manager, who will be faced with the training of personnel, possible reorganization of music library and other materials, and technical execution.

GRANT, the promotion manager, who will face a major assignment in publicizing the new format.

> THE CASE STUDY PROBLEM: As Burns, develop an overall plan that will meet all aspects and implications of Grainger's challenge—"A good station, a solid station, a significant voice in the community."

A Special Note

For the individual studying the case, the involvement of all six persons should be studied through other sources, and a final conclusion drawn.

However, in a classroom or seminar situation, it might be more interesting to assign the roles of the six executives to various participants—with the suggested outside reading to be used as reinforcement for their individual decisions. It should be remembered that Burns, as station manager, will have an overruling vote —for the simple and the practical reason that *he* must bear the responsibility for the results!

SUGGESTED READINGS

(12) Quaal and Brown — chapter 3 ("Radio station programming").
(16) Stanley — various readings under "Radio."
(17) Stanley and Steinberg — various readings under "Radio" and "Radio programming."

4

"PAID RELIGION: DO YOU OR DON'T YOU?"

When we sing a song about God's gospel we don't vaguely mention the product. We go all the way. We were trained on that. When you got a good horse you don't trade him in for a dud. You stay with him.

> Howard Goodman, patriarch of the Goodman family's *God and Country Spectacular*

The voice of religion in the United States has made an electronic presence since 1920, in radio's earliest experimental days. *The Eternal Light,* Father Coughlin, Norman Vincent Peale, Ralph Sockman, *The Lutheran Hour, The Protestant Hour,* are but a modest sampling of the sounds of radio's heyday. And Bishop Fulton J. Sheen, in the pioneering DuMont TV network days of the late '40s and early '50s, set a pattern for the cult of personality that has persisted and grown in paid video religious broadcasts.

"Paid" is the key word in today's religious broadcasting. While *The National Radio Pulpit* was among the best known of public service (meaning free) offerings in radio, it's the purchased-time fundamentalist thunder of Graham, Roberts, Humbard and Shuller that dominates religious television today—most often backed up by radio (*Hour of Decision,* Carl McIntyre, etc.) in its overall thrust.

The reason for buying time for religion is simple and obvious: when you pay, you get—with some limitations—pretty much what you want. When you come asking, biretta, fedora or yamulkah in hand, you get slotted in the ghetto of Sunday early morning; or, at best, in the "who-watches" intellectual ghetto of early Sunday afternoon.

And—if you are the Southern Baptist Convention, the Catholic producers of *The Christophers,* the Lutheran producers of *Davey and Goliath,* any of the four Protestant bodies sharing production of *The Protestant Hour,* or any other of the major faith suppliers of public service programming for the broadcast industry —you nod humbly, and thank the industry for being so gracious in its gift of free time.

Even if you can't find evidence that anybody's out there!

The powerful Graham organization, however, wants to know that not just anybody but many, many viewers are out there when a *Crusade* is televised; expertly videotapes the consecutive evenings of a campaign and ships them on to major market TV stations— where prime time has been purchased on solid independent or even network affiliate video outlets. Compelling newspaper ads, tune-in reminders in *TV Guide,* billboards and direct mail all are employed to promote viewing.

How does Dr. Graham afford this? Two million dollars to be on 25 eastern seaboard outlets for five nights during one *Crusade?* Exact figures are difficult to come by, but estimates have it that the Graham group draws from a minimum of $2 up to $5 in mail response for every dollar invested in time and production. "P&G never did so well," muses a veteran ad agency president.

The paid-religion dollar is tempting to the broadcaster. "Money in the bank, and one step closer to heaven at the same time," a critic wrote in the late 1940s. Yet there are pitfalls. Once a station accepts paid-time religion, it can hardly be selective in accommodating the evangelizing zeal of a Roberts or a Graham while denying the privilege of paid exposure to other groups with political axes to grind in their messages: second-generation versions of the religious radio that offered "Illuminated bibles with the true

Paid Religion: Do You or Don't You?

word" for 79 cents and "Handkerchiefs guaranteed dipped in the holy water at Lourdes."

The viewer or listener responds to an offering of literature through the station facilities, and finds himself on a list for "hate" propaganda of one sort or another; or is bombarded by and billed for unrequested books and even libraries of dubious literature in which he has no interest; or is called on by persistent salespeople . . .

To what degree are you, the broadcaster, liable?

By the very nature of being a sometime originator and always relayer of messages to a mass audience, the broadcaster is to some extent inured to slings and arrows. In any given month the manager is apt to hear from a range of partisan interests including the Girl Scouts, the Audubon Society and the Pop Werner League, all protesting some real or fancied slight to their cause.

But in the broad category of religion the broadcaster has a special kind of nervousness. An adamant churchman has succeeded in pulling the license of a southern station; others appear before the FCC and congressional committees at every opportunity, mostly with damning opinions on the performances of networks and stations vis-a-vis their interests.

The station operator can't—or doesn't feel able to—afford to employ a religion specialist on the staff; yet that operator isn't certain of the advice of the local ministerial association or council of churches.

Yet the license, the franchise to operate, is in his hands. *What to do about religious broadcasting?*

The 1977 meeting of National Religious Broadcasters, Inc., dominant group of broadcast outlets and groups specializing in fulltime paid religious broadcasting, announced that an average of one new radio station per week is being licensed for this purpose. And TV stations—primarily UHF—are reported to be joining the fold.

Particularly in a market where one of these stations is airing hard-sell gospel messages day and night, at commercial rates, the conservative station manager sees money that might be his go elsewhere. But if he succumbs to the angelic voices of the four-square gospel advertisers, what happens to his relationship with the "Mainline" Protestant denominations, the Roman Catholic broadcast office, the Jewish groups?

THE CASE STUDY: *Formulating a firm policy on religious broadcasting for the local station is the subject of this case study.* Do you *or* Don't you *is the hard bottom line.*

SUGGESTED READINGS

(1) Bluem — many general readings; also "Guidelines for the religious program planner" and "A short history of religious broadcasting."
(2) Brown — see "Religious broadcasting."
(5) Ellens — general readings for background and policy formulation.
(12) Quaal and Brown — see reference under "Radio station programming."

5

"A STITCH IN TIME SAVES SEVEN"

Station WAAA is one of three TV outlets (all network affiliates) in a market of 350,000 TV households. In the eastern time zone, it carries regular network programming up to 11:00 p.m.; following its 11–11:30 local block of programming, it rejoins the network for the nighttime personality show.

The 11:00 p.m. local period, under the overall title of SEVEN at ELEVEN, is offered seven nights a week (substitute talent on Saturdays or Sundays). The program details are these:

   11:00—*News Roundup*—Clifford Allen
   11:15—*Weather*—Mel Grimes
   11:20—*Features 'n' Fun*—Maggi Hurd
   11:25—*Sports*—Laddy Trent

Now that's what the program detail *was,* but not quite what it *is.* The five-times-a-year audience estimates from both rating services offer 11:00 p.m. and 11:30 entries; within that 30-minute time span and following a general trend, WAAA has to some extent mixed subject matter (and personalities) according to importance —but *to some extent* is the key. As noted below, many local clients are firm in their identity with one or another of the TV spokespeople, and won't stand for any significant change.

THE BACKGROUND

The SEVEN at ELEVEN format (an almost universal one in local station programming, granting minor modifications) has been in existence since the air date of WAAA: three of the four personalities—Allen, Grimes, Hurd—have been on the air for over 10 years; Trent, while newer, is a former star halfback from the local university and is equally well known.

The program block has been a solid income-producing feature for the station since its introduction. (Historical as well as capital expense note: the station built new facilities nine years ago, including the "Million Dollar Studio"—only a slight bit of poetic license in titling the area in which SEVEN at ELEVEN production takes place, because the program segment is responsible for close to a million dollars in annual billing.)

SEVEN at ELEVEN has been dominant in the rating reports of two major audience measurement services for a like period of time. Channel Four has made repeated attempts—with new talent and formats, with extensive promotion campaigns—to achieve the number one spot, but has continued in a respectable and mostly saleable number two position. The third station, Channel 10, has not competed seriously in the time period.

The Problem

WAAA station manager Roy Murphy is forced to a serious re-evaluation of the situation when a series of rumblings and complaints come to him over a period of several weeks, all pointing to rating problems and selling difficulties concerned with SEVEN at ELEVEN.

The first note of alarm comes from the sales manager of the sales representative firm in New York: "What's happening out there, Roy? This is the fifth book (rating report) in a row with Maggi and Trent going downhill. Any more, and we lose the toothpaste and the food guys—unless you want to cut the rates, that is!"

Murphy promises to check the situation; the next day receives a memo from his local sales manager. "You know that First Savings and Loan has a long-standing interest in Cliff Allen—they've been on with him for eight years, on alternate nights with the utility people. But we're being sniped at by Channel Four. They are coming *up;* we are going *down.* Unless we do something to check this, we are going to lose one or two good clients—or at least they are going to cut back to a couple of nights a week and put part of their money over on Four. What ammunition have you got for me to use in meeting this?"

A few days later, Murphy's program manager arrives with a related problem. "Laddy Trent has a proposal. Next fall, he wants to take off from Thursday through Monday each week—during the NCAA football season—to go out and cover the final practices, the games and the post-mortems at the top college games, by national standards. And he says that he can get almost all of the travel and filming and what-not paid for.

"I've told him that we can't afford, and *he* can't afford, to be away during the October-November rating period, but he says that the interviews and the films he'll bring back will make his weeknight programs twice as attractive. And that he can produce some post-season special programs from the films. And that, of course, he doesn't like ratings anyway. What do *you* say?"

Murphy sighed, shook his head: "You're correct, of course— we can't have him away from his show for half the nights of a major rating period. Our competition and their sales reps would noise this all over. Tell him that—and when he howls and comes to me, I'll reinforce it."

The following week, the station promotion manager had a luncheon lament for Murphy. "Maggi Hurd is talent, and a female, and a bit of a prima donna, and everybody in my department knows this and plays the game. But she's getting too hard to work with—misses a press interview without an apology, won't pose for the usual gag pictures for Halloween—says that as women's director for the station this is beneath her position—and gives us a lot of guff before she agrees to take the usual client promotions and interviews that we put her show together for in the first place."

To complete the talent problem for the full half-hour period, Weatherman Mel Grimes threw his own gripes to Murphy: "I'm simply not getting either the production *or* promotional support needed. I've seen tapes of that girl they're using to do weather over on Four, and she has all kinds of spinning devices and electronic aids to make the show look good. We are still doing what we did 10 years ago. *And,* your promotion man does nothing to support me—the spots on the air hardly ever appear, and I haven't seen a *TV Guide* ad in months!"

Seeking a Solution

At this point, Murphy sat back to take a careful reading of the situation. He was well aware of the slipping ratings, and potential loss of clients and revenue. For much of the past year, he had worked with his program and promotion managers, trying to find ways to freshen the programs and to reverse the downward ratings trend.

But he faced a difficult problem in carrying the story to Mark Marius, his vice president and general manager.

Marius, a one-time orchestra leader and show producer, carries a monumental reputation as a programmer in network radio, and brought his "show biz" magic to television. As assistant general manager of WAAA, he had created the format of SEVEN at ELEVEN when the TV station went on the air; had selected, coached and guided three of the four current stars; thought of and still thinks of the 30-minute period as his very own idea. Murphy had learned from his first days as a WAAA salesman that *Mark's Monsters* were in a very special category—to be protected, promoted, and *not* to be criticized.

Murphy's secretary groaned: "I don't envy you, having to take this one to Mr. Marius!"

With no little fear of the outcome, Murphy laid the problem before Marius. He was surprised at the reception: "Yeah, I read those rating books too, and I knew you'd get a lot of pressure. Well, I don't think much of ratings, unless they put me on first. Don't like 'em; never did; think we'd all be a lot better off without 'em." He spun his chair around, grunted to his secretary: "Get me Jack Seaton at ABX."

(Seaton, a well-known radio and TV audience measurement researcher, is head of ABX Services, best known and most-often-used local rating service—also the one in which SEVEN at ELEVEN has taken its most severe drop.)

Marius moved immediately to the business at hand: "Jack, my station manager, Roy Murphy, is with me, and he tells me that we have a problem with the 11:00 p.m. ratings. Could you come out here sometime soon and straighten us out on this?"

With a date and time set, Marius hung up and concluded to

Murphy: "Don't worry—he'll work out some changes, and we'll all be in good shape in a couple of months."

With somewhat less conviction in the outcome, Murphy left to draw up details for the staff meeting with Seaton.

At the meeting, Seaton came armed with an assistant plus a carrying case of large charts. The WAAA management group, with Marius and Murphy at the head, included the national and local sales managers, the program manager, the promotion, news and business managers. Marius opened the session: "Jack is here at my invitation, to give us some details on the SEVEN at ELEVEN problems that some people think we have. He knows what I think about it, so I won't repeat anything here, but just let him go ahead. Jack, all we want is better ratings!"

Seaton, with a smile, did indeed go ahead. "First of all, permit me to review just what we do to get those so-called magic figures, or funny numbers, depending on where you stand at the moment. We can't phone or send diaries to all 500,000 television households in your area for each rating period, so we sample a portion of those households. Now I know that it seems like a very small sample—but at the same time neither you nor your competitors would be willing to pay for the operation of a sampling at 10 times, or even four times, the present rate. Nor do we think that necessary.

"If we are doing the job of random sampling to the best of our ability, then the results should be projectable to your total market with reasonable accuracy—as you well know, we always insert cautionary notes that these sampling techniques are subject to a certain margin of error."

"Not until recently," Marius interjected, with a small chuckle from his staff in response.

"Exactly so, Mark," Seaton continued. He turned to his first chart—a zigzag graphing of WAAA audiences as opposed to the other two stations, for the 11:00 and 11:30 p.m. periods and running across a ten-year span.

"You can see here the SEVEN at ELEVEN story for the past 10 years. It has entered the time period with a dominant share of the audience; has held a greater percentage of audience throughout the half-hour; has led into the late night network show with more audience than the other two stations together—*up to this year.*"

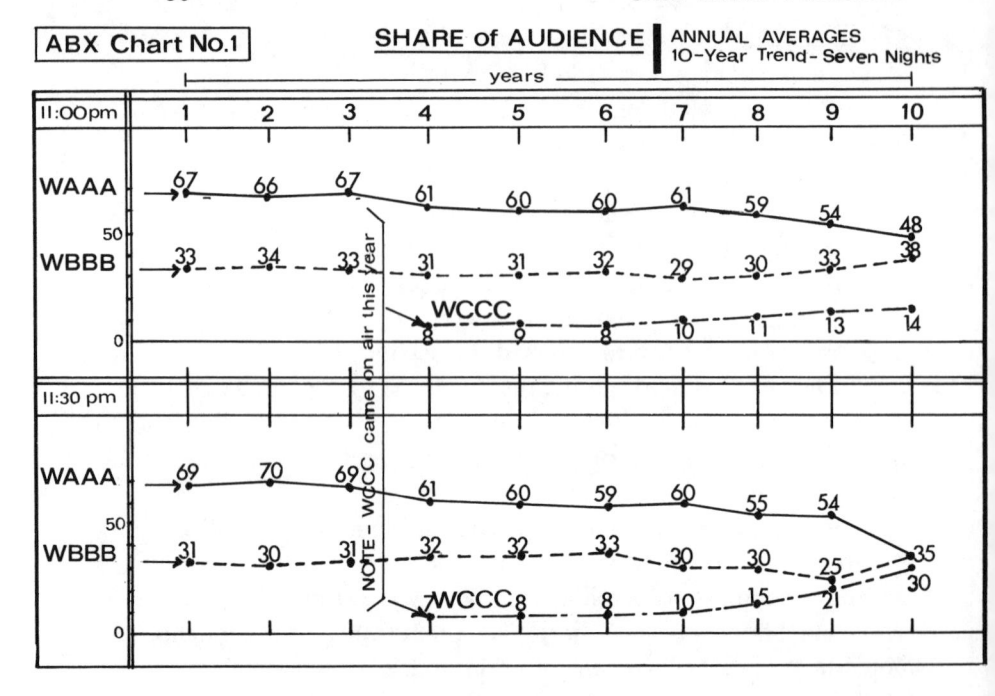

ABX Chart No.1 — SHARE of AUDIENCE
ANNUAL AVERAGES — 10-Year Trend - Seven Nights

11:00 pm

years	1	2	3	4	5	6	7	8	9	10
WAAA	67	66	67	61	60	60	61	59	54	48
WBBB	33	34	33	31	31	32	29	30	33	38
WCCC				8	9	8	10	11	13	14

NOTE — WCCC came on air this year (at year 4)

11:30 pm

WAAA	69	70	69	61	60	59	60	55	54	35
WBBB	31	30	31	32	32	33	30	30	25	30/35
WCCC				8	8	10	15	21		

Seaton went on: "But that's history now. Let's look at the past 10 months, when there have been five four-week report periods published for your market. Here is the trend, like it or not. You are bit-by-bit losing your share of audience, while Four is gaining and Ten is as well. Project this trend for another season, and you are then in the position that Four was in two years ago."

Marius interrupted with some heat: "Everybody knows that you take these ratings with just a few hundred people—they could all be Channel Four viewers! How do you know?"

Seaton was patient in replying. "Mark, we grant many possibilities of error and bias in sampling—but this can be as good or as bad for one station in a market as another. Any *one* of these five rating periods could have error in it, but the overall trend running through almost a full year can't be written off as continuing error and continuing bias *against* you and *for* your competition. To be brutally frank, your programming is failing you!"

The room was silent. "Let me go ahead," Seaton continued, signaling for a third chart.

doubtful about carrying it off with the present talent. Maggi, for one, is in my thinking over-exposed on the station. She does her daytime half-hour shows; she's on tape with commercials for six different sponsors at all hours of the day and night; she's on our radio station with tape commercials as well. I just don't think she has anything more to add to this nighttime program block—*if* we need a woman in here, let's get a new one!"

Bain, the local sales manager, was next: "Roy, two points. First, I know that everybody thinks Maggi and Mel are the weakest links in what we have to offer, and I'll be the first to admit that weather could be given in 30 seconds and that girly-type interviews and features are pretty light stuff. But these two people are the best sales and promotion gimmicks we have to work with at the local level; they go out and meet clients, they do interviews with them and go to their lunches and company picnics, and they have a personal knowledge of the products they're selling.

"Second—and it really ties in with my first point—if we don't have separate shows for these people, we don't have any real way to sell them to local clients!"

News Manager Olsen cut in: "We simply have to offer news as news, or come off second best as a primary source of news reporting for the public. Also, I'd like to know how we can claim adequate periods of news reporting for the FCC if we don't have programs identified as such?"

Court, the business manager, was next: "Financially, this new concept implies added production and overhead—it would have to carry a full load of commercial announcements *each and every week,* summer as well as winter, to pay its way at the present level. These talent people have been with us a long time, and are all being paid top money for their work. I don't think that they would accept less money because we decide to give them less exposure during parts of the week or month or year.

"All-in-all, we might be better off to retain the present format, but find some fresh—and less-expensive—people, to do it. And I *do* recognize the danger of our talent going over to Channel Ten—but I don't think they are ready over there to pay them!"

Carling answered: "Our people have other program commitments, and contracts that are flexible enough to keep them happy. As a matter of fact, this anticipates my second proposal—that we program the same format at 6:30 p.m., on a Monday-through-Friday basis, as another part of an "All-new concept in local information' promotion."

Ness, the promotion manager, spoke: "Don't forget that you are asking for a lot of additional promotion time and money when you consider either or both of these new half-hours."

"But we'd have to do that anyway," Murphy replied, "If we put new people in the present format."

Richards responded with enthusiasm: "For the national spot business, the early evening half-hour in this new format, packaged with the 11:00 p.m. period, might create some excitement in the New York agencies. We could come up with some seasonal sales plans to cover *both* early and late periods, and rotate spots for maximum reach and frequency."

Bain groaned: "An early as well as late block in this new format would only compound local sales problems. The pattern among most of our local clients is to buy a personality and a show, even if it's only five minutes one night a week. My boys sell Maggi and Mel and Cliff and Laddy as personalities—*not* rotating positions. They—the clients—use their pictures in store promotions, and have an identity with them. What we really need are better ratings for saleable personalities."

Murphy offered a reminder: "Under our present programming, over the broadcast day and week, our other-than-network income is about 65% national spot, 35% local—which is about average for our type of market. To move one way might seem to offer more availability for national business; to stand pat in format would seem to ask for more local advertising."

Richards replied: "Let me hedge my comments this way—I think Joe's new plan has the possibility of attracting a lot of additional national spot money *if*—and I admit that's a big *if*—it in turn attracts a very substantial share of the audience."

To which Bain added: "And unless that audience increase is *very* substantial, we would stand to lose a sizeable amount of local billing—at least in terms of present clients. Maybe we could go out and get others—and we'd most certainly try—but there would be some light billing periods before we regained even what we have now."

Murphy turned to Ness, his promotion man. "Any one of these propositions, or a combination of any, would demand a lot of promotion, as you have pointed out. Could you come up with a rough guess on costs?"

"I hope fairly close," Ness answered. "Fortunately, we have the staff for the job. However, our advertising and promotion budget is pretty much geared for and adequate to our present operation. Something like this demands a real all-out *burst*—lots of print advertising, billboards, bus cards and the rest. We'd probably want to run a contest or two, with big prizes. There'd be press parties, and advertiser parties, and personal appearances. Our sales rep would certainly want a special presentation in New York. All in all, I'd hang a 50-to-60 thousand supplementary—meaning *not* in the budget—price tag on a 13-week campaign."

Murphy nodded: "Let's bear that in mind."

"But we'll need additional promotion, even if we stay with our present people and format," Carling said.

"No argument," Murphy replied. "The question becomes one of where we are going to spend it for the maximum result.

"At this stage," Murphy continued, "let's have a change of pace. So far, I've led you pretty much in the area of program concept—whether to make a dramatic shift or to stand firm with what we have, on more or less traditional forms. We've heard some honest, even blunt, evaluations of what all of this might mean on the national spot and local sales levels. And we've run through production and promotional costs, and the potential of news crediting in a legal sense.

"We've had a number of opinions on the personalities involved; but now I'd like to take them one at a time, to get some idea of your thinking as to their present and future value to us. I'll name them, and anybody who wants to—shoot out whatever comment you have.

"First, CLIFF ALLEN." "Smart guy, came out of the local university sociology faculty, but not really a TV-type newsman by present standards . . . Solid man, better than most markets this size can put on the air . . . A little gray at the temples in comparison to the competition . . . But that's good for the reliable news image . . . A little bit aloof with clients—he goes out to the lunches and factory tours, but he doesn't seem to have his heart in it . . . Gives a dignified, news-with-authority appearance . . ."

"Next we have MEL GRIMES—and let me add that he talked to me recently about visual effects and ways to upgrade the program." "Mel hasn't had any professional training—we grabbed him from the newsroom way back, because he'd been in Air Force meteorology school and knew the words, and he still sounds like an amateur . . . But that's part of his charm—weather is a silly subject anyway, and he makes it entertaining . . . How about a female with some curvier isotherms for visual effect? . . . I wonder if the weather is really worth a five-minute program every night?". . .

"And then we come to our women's director and nighttime feature personality, MAGGI HURD." "Overexposed; on the air too much . . . But she still has a great following in the area . . . Like Cliff, she's getting a little gray at the edges; *if* we continue to have a female with a feature insert at night, maybe it should be somebody with a little more appeal for the younger boys in the audience . . . I don't think we should have a woman at all—it causes resentment among women in the audience, and this is part of our ratings problem . . . Maggi is just a little *too* sophisticated and well-groomed—my wife says she can't stand the comparison at 11:20 p.m.!". . .

"And, finally, LADDY TRENT with sports." "A nice boy, but I sometimes wonder whether the subject is worth a five-minute segment on a year-'round basis. Lots of times he seems to be filling time with scores nobody cares about *here,* and with news items about soccer and polo players and whatnot . . . The saloon crowd thinks he's the greatest—if we dropped him, I think we'd lose a lot of hard-core audience . . . Sports *may* be worth a show every night, but I wonder if we couldn't do it a lot less expensively with more pictures and a staff news guy?". . .

"Okay," Murphy concluded, "we've looked at programming and at the people in the time period. We've explored the commercial problems, and the probable outcomes of various shifts. We've all been with it long enough to know that there's no point in conjuring up wild changes—we *do* need a solid block of profitable local programming in the time period. From here on, I have to boil down your thoughts, and try to come up with some reasonable suggestions and plans for Mark. Thanks, and I'll keep you posted."

"A Stitch in Time Saves Seven" 61

| ABX Chart No. 2 | SHARE of AUDIENCE | FIVE CONSECUTIVE PERIODS OVER 10 MONTHS... |

measurement periods

11:00 pm	— 1 —	— 2 —	— 3 —	— 4 —	— 5 —
WAAA	51	49	50	48	46
WBBB	34	35	34	36	39
WCCC	15	16	16	16	15

11:30 pm					
WAAA	44	36	37	37	36
WBBB	31	33	34	34	35
WCCC	25	31	29	29	29

"Here is a composite—an averaging of these last five report periods, showing the performance of each of your four programs in your SEVEN at ELEVEN period against your competition. You know that we don't claim to have a large enough sample to break down five-minute programs, as you have between 11:15 and 11:30, for any *one* rating period. But over the five cycles we *can* do it, and here it is for you, including a comparison to the same periods as averaged for a year earlier."

Seaton went on to analyze the new chart: "In the first 15-minute period, all three stations have a news segment. This is the easiest to compare. Your Cliff Allen has dropped slightly, but in lesser proportion than the last half of the period. To some extent, you might even be able to defend this in terms of a lesser lead-in from network programming, on two or three nights of the week.

"But it does remain that the curve is down.

"The next five minutes has a common denominator of weather programming, and here you can see that Grimes drops five points below the preceding quarter-hour, and is only three points above his major competition.

CASE STUDY PROBLEMS

ABX Chart No. 3 — **COMPOSITE COMPARISON** — AVERAGE OF FIVE PERIODS FOR PREVIOUS & CURRENT YEARS — Sun-Sat averages

TIME / STATION	CH.	PROGRAM	CURRENT YEAR (+) average for 5 periods Met. Rtng.	HH's (000)	PREVIOUS YEAR (++) average for 5 periods Met. Rtng.	HH's (000)
11:00 pm						
WAAA	7	C. ALLEN NEWS	20	102	23	113
WBBB	4	Local News	16	81	14	69
WCCC	10	Local News	6	28	5	24
11:15 pm						
WAAA	7	M. GRIMES – WEA	15	74	19	93
WBBB	4	Weather	12	61	10	50
WCCC	10	Weather	4	21	3	15
11:20 pm						
WAAA	7	M. HURD – FEA	9	45	14	67
WBBB	4	News Spec	9	45	7	34
WCCC	10	Movie	6	29	4	20
11:25 pm						
WAAA	7	L. TRENT – SPR	8	41	13	63
WBBB	4	News Spec	8	41	6	29
WCCC	10	Movie	7	33	5	24

(+) Current Year — 500,000 TV Household Base
(++) Previous Year — 482,000 TV Household Base

"The next five minutes has no common denominator—your Maggi Hurd feature stands against a special local news feature on Four, and the early start of a movie on Ten. Actually, when you take this five minute period by itself, she is tied with the programming on Four.

"The last five minutes drops another rating point, but continues in a dead heat with the corresponding drop on Four.

"To face the situation, you have to note that it is only because the second 15 minutes are normally reported in one block of time that you are not indicated as close to a tie."

Marius spoke: "Yeah, but Maggi has always had a good audience, and she gets a lot of mail—and the clients love her."

"Love her," Murphy added, "but a couple of them are threatening to drop her."

"Look, Mark," Seaton went on, "I want to leave this material with you, and I hope you'll consider it for the good research that I believe it is. I make no claims for infallibility, but I do think that you should weigh this carefully. I'll say again that we can be wrong in one period or another; but I'll also repeat that the evidence over a longer period of time has to have weight. I don't know your operation in enough detail, nor is it my job to say whether I think you need new personalities, or new visual effects and set designs, or more promotion, or what. But I will say that I am convinced that you need to take action to correct your problems. At our end, all we can do is report what we find."

After routine thank yous and farewells, Seaton and his assistant left and the conference room was silent.

"Look, Mark," Murphy began . . .

"It's okay, Roy," Marius cut in. "I know how to read handwriting on walls. But I'm too close to this to make any smart decisions. Kick it around with these guys, and in a couple of weeks I'd like some proposals on what to do."

Marius stood up, and continued: "Do remember this—we've invested a lot of time, and development, and money, in these stars of ours. They're known all over town, and to New York agency people as well. I don't want an easy answer that will send them over to Channel Ten so that we can be cut down even more!"

After Marius left the room, it exploded: "We've got to get a new news guy, and fast! . . . Maggi pulls the whole thing down with the feature show . . . Let's get some new gimmicks in the weather!" . . .

Murphy rose, held up his hands: "Okay, but no more today. I'll have copies made of all this stuff that Jack brought us. You have the sales figures, the projections, and the list of current clients. This is Tuesday. Friday morning we start a long, maybe all-day meeting, to lock horns and to come to some conclusions. Remember what Mark just said, and don't make snap judgments—I want solid thinking and sensible ideas. Programming is *it,* so Joe and I will review and put up a first proposal, if only to have something to knock down. Where we go from there depends on what everybody else has to offer, but here are two points: first, I want to push this with Mark well before his two-week deadline, as do you; second, I'll order lunch brought in. Goodbye!"

When the Friday meeting began, Murphy had agreed to the broad-scale revision in programming offered by Joe Carling, his program manager, as a "first proposal."

"What you see here," Murphy began, "is a large target in the shape of a preliminary programming plan—for shooting at with whatever weapons you have. We will tape the whole meeting; will edit and transcribe by common agreement, and will submit to Mark what I hope will be a reasonably concise statement of majority opinion—with the thinking to back it up. Joe, you take over . . ."

Carling, the program manager, showed a programming plan. "I would like to suggest a complete shuffle of the people and the ingredients of what we now have, and retain the concept of SEVEN at ELEVEN. This would be a 30-minute show, completely flexible. Cliff Allen would be the overall moderator or communicator or host or whatever; the other people would go in and out with materials according to the timeliness and importance of the subject. In the tight period of August and September, Laddy Trent would come in very early in the program with baseball action among the top teams in both leagues. He'd do the same in the latter parts of the collegiate and professional football seasons, and for other major sports. When the sports action was light, his participation would be light as well.

"Mel Grimes would do the same with weather. When the subject was new snow records or hurricanes, he'd be on right after the opening; with everything normal, he'd be brief, and come on late in the program with the forecast.

"Maggi would be in and out, with one- or two-minute interviews and features.

"And we'd add a straight newsman for local stuff—with the obvious understanding that, all through the show, we'd be as visual as possible with films and stills of all kinds."

"So now we have something to shoot at," Murphy added. "I want to amplify the commercial reasoning behind this proposal: it retains the present talent, and the investment we have in them; it offers the promotional possibilities of a new concept in programming for our area; it makes available the flexibility of carrying spot announcements, national *or* local, throughout the show, without tying us to any single sponsor or co-sponsorship arrangement—and the obvious pressures that those agreements imply.

"So," Murphy smiled, "who's first in the duck blind?"

Richards, the national sales manager, spoke: "I like the concept, and I think our sales rep would feel the same way. But I'm

THE CASE STUDY PROBLEM: As Roy Murphy, write a comprehensive report to general manager Marius, with a detailed program format *and* the reasoning for the decisions.

SUGGESTED READINGS

(12) Quaal and Brown — chapter 4 ("Audience research").
(14) Roe — chapter 7 ("The broadcast day") and chapter 13 ("Revenue" and "Sales analyses").
(16) Stanley — selective readings under "The station in a lagging market."

6

MEET MOLLY
ALBATROSS OR GOLDEN GOOSE?

THE BACKGROUND

Molly Heatherstone has been a daytime fixture of Channel Four for over 10 years—the glib hostess-interviewer of *Meet Molly,* a 30-minute Monday-through-Friday series that combines glimpses of visiting celebrities, songs and instrumental numbers by a small group, "editorial" mentions of new products being advertised on the show, and a very full roster of clients, mostly national advertisers but a few from the local market as well.

For the past three years Molly's husband (and manager), Harvey, has appeared on the show on Tuesdays and Thursdays with short commentaries on news and current events.

Originally a studio program, *Meet Molly* became a mobile troupe with the addition of new station technical equipment: for live appearances, at shopping plaza openings, state and county fairs, clients' shops and factories, and for videotaping of events for later use, Molly has had the mobile van and supporting equipment in use two or three days of every week.

The popularity of the show—Molly in sensible shoes, tweed suits and occasional Boston lady hats, and Harvey, also a little tweedy and with a British guardsman mustache—seems guaranteed; the list of clients solid and satisfied.

Competition has never been a problem: In a four-station market of approximately one million households, *Meet Molly* gathers about 100,000 households on the average, compared to Channel Seven's *Hostess Time* with 80,000 later in the day, and

Meet Molly . . . Albatross or Golden Goose?

to Channel Ten's *Food 'n' Fun,* offered still later and running a poor third with about 30,000 households. The fourth station has no program in the category.

The Problem

With this background common knowledge, it was a very real bombshell dropped when Channel Four station manager Jim White stated to his staff: "I'm giving very serious thought to dropping *Meet Molly*—talent, format, mobile activity, the whole thing!"

The announcement came near the end of two full days of program, operation and sales review by White and his department heads. The meeting had been initiated by the top management of the group station ownership—with the very strong suggestion that, even though Channel Four was in a dominant market position, all avenues be explored to make certain that dominance was retained, and that cost of operation be held in line.

There had been a number of suggestions made, and decisions either agreed upon or tabled for review after the fall season had been run through, at least to the first of the year.

But *Meet Molly* seemed so invulnerable a part of the daytime schedule that it hadn't been mentioned by any member of the group.

"Now let me go on before you explode," White said with a smile. "I didn't say flatly that I was going to do it—I said that I'm giving it serious thought. And this is the major reason I asked Ben Warren to come out from our New York sales representative office. I'm sure that he and Lou, as national sales manager, will have some violent objections, and I want the thing to be turned over completely before any action is taken."

Warren shook his head. "Jim, you can't be serious. In New York, Molly is one of the easiest sales we have to make. My guys would go into shock if you took her off."

"All too true, Jim," Lou Linz cut in. "When I'm on agency calls with Ben and his people, that's one time period we never have to make a pitch on. They just want to know if they can get in."

"She's a great place to plant interviews with traveling promotion people for new products—really gives them the red carpet treatment," the promotion manager added.

"Which in turn makes her all the easier to sell the next time around," Warren said.

"From a local point of view, we couldn't care," the local sales manager said. "She's too expensive, and a little too high-toned in her personal relations with local agencies and advertisers. We sell her once in a while, but mostly as a daytime spot for somebody doing shotgun buying through the local schedule. We'd have to have a lower rate card and a lot more loving cooperation before she'd ever be a prime item with my contacts."

White held up his hand. "I've got to explain some things, particularly to Ben and Lou, so they don't think I've stacked the meeting. May, and Frank, and Maurie"—he nodded in turn to three of his department heads, May Higgens, women's director, Frank Simmons, business manager, and Maurie Shafer, program manager—"have known my concern about Molly, and have helped me gather some interesting information. Maurie . . ."

"The network began to blow the whistle on Molly a year ago," Shafer stated, "when we moved the show back a half-hour because of the soap opera shift. They pointed out that wherever Molly ran she gave them a poor lead-in for the network program that followed . . ."

"Let the network worry about it," Warren muttered.

"That's a good theory up to a point," Shafer answered, "but we thought that it might just have a lesson for us as well. So we had both of the rating services do some special studies for us. I've summarized a few of the most important areas on these three charts in front of you.

"We all know," he continued, "or at least we've always said, that Molly has a great women's audience. Women-women-women—the shoppers and buyers and controllers of the purse strings. And if you don't believe it"—Shafer grinned—"just read some of the flow of promotion copy that George turns out of his department!

"But we face a problem. The rating services are producing more and more demographic detailing of *who's* in the audience—not just women as a single category, but young and middle-aged and older women, and women in different income groups and working women and women with and without kids of school age.

"And they're beginning to cross-ruff this stuff with details about who buys what, and how much.

Meet Molly . . . Albatross or Golden Goose? 73

MOLLY – CHART No.1

WOMEN VIEWERS ▬
Mon–Fri Average Audience –(000)

Channel Program Time	Total Women	Women by Age Groups		
		18-34	35-49	50+
Ch.4 **MEET MOLLY** 1–1:30 pm	(0 0 0) 89	(0 0 0) 24	(0 0 0) 26	(0 0 0) 39
Ch.7 **Hostess Time** 3–3:30 pm	73	29	27	17
Ch.10 **Food 'n' Fun** 4–4:30 pm	27	9	10	8

"In this first chart our Molly doesn't come off so well. She has a very respectable number under 'women'—but when you break those gals into age categories you see that she is weakest in the youngest group, average in the middle group, and has a big margin with the ladies over 50!"

Ben Warren interrupted: "Maurie, I'm forced to admit that you have some point. We've had a little resistance from a couple of the big agencies—the guys who use computers in place of time buyers and whatnot. But it's still not a problem."

"Be patient, there's more," Shafer answered. "Our second chart examines a very special category of the women's audience, the Lady of the House, the gal who holds the pursestrings, does the shopping, and the rest of it. The ratings people are able to break down just *who* she is in a number of ways, as you see here—by the presence or absence of children in the household, and also by the size of that household.

"Once again we have problems with Molly. She does indeed command more Lady of the House types than her competition, but

MOLLY – CHART No.2

LADY of the HOUSE VIEWERS

Mon–Fri Average Audience – (000)

Channel Program Time	Total Lady of House	Lady of House by Categories			
		No Children in House	Youngest Under 6	Youngest 6–17	Family 5 or More
Ch.4 **MEET MOLLY** 1–1:30 pm	(000) 81	(000) 37	(000) 18	(000) 26	(000) 13
Ch.7 **Hostess Time** 3–3:30 pm	69	13	32	24	21
Ch.10 **Food 'n' Fun** 4–4:30 pm	24	6	10	8	9

who are they? In the category of *no children in house*—which we can for the most part interpret as those ladies over 50—she is on top, but you can see that she isn't dominant in the next two categories, and is a poor second in the *five-or-more* family size group, where the food and drug people want to make most of their sales."

Ben Warren nodded: "I'd be a bad sales rep for you if I didn't admit that this is the area where we have begun to find a little resistance. But I still don't think it's enough of a problem to kill a program that gives off the aura of a winner!"

Shafer smiled: "I don't like to advocate knocking off winners either. But let's turn to the third chart—here you see another area where your national buyers are taking a hard look at the overall audience—the *cumulative* audience—the number of households tuning to a program at least once over a period of weeks. This is the largest stumbling block for the future—Molly has a large but static viewership, and in four weeks she reaches less homes than her principal competition, and in eight weeks considerably less, close to 50,000 less. Can you fight this?"

Shafer sat down as White spoke: "We don't have to find arguments for those data at the moment, if only for the reason that

Meet Molly . . . Albatross or Golden Goose?

there are some other considerations. A very major one is what Molly has done and has the promise of doing for us in the future, in terms of her relations with her—and our—public. May Higgens has done a lot of searching on this, and I'd like to turn the floor over to her."

"No charts," May said, "but some observations. Molly has a great acceptance in our market. We have a continuing flow of requests for tickets to her studio shows, and she always gathers crowds at her remote tapings. We have ten times more requests than we can possibly accommodate for her guest interviews—women's clubs sponsoring art shows and P-TA's holding carnivals and men's groups selling Christmas trees for charity and all the rest.

"But this very personal contact type of activity is a dead give-away to the make-up of the audience. And what I see, and what we handle in the mail, most definitely backs up Maurie's research studies. These girls may still giggle, but they do it while encased in middle-to-large girdles, and in some cases through suspiciously even sets of teeth!"

White brought the meeting back to order: "We've had both the reports of our audience research friends and the candid ap-

MOLLY – CHART No. 3

EIGHT-WEEK CUMULATIVE AUDIENCE
Number & Percent of Total Households Reached at Least Once

Channel Program Time	Average Week Rating Households	4-Wk. Cume Households		8-Wk. Cume Households	
	% (OOO)	(OOO)	%Total HHs	(OOO)	%Total HHs
Ch. 4 **MEET MOLLY** 1-1:30 pm	10 99	107	11	113	11
Ch. 7 **Hostess Time** 3-3:30pm	8 81	123	12	149	15
Ch. 10 **Food 'n' Fun** 4-4:30pm	3 29	41	4	63	6

praisal of an eyewitness reporter. Now I'd like you to hear the business side from Frank Simmons."

"I'm sure you realize this," Simmons began, "but just for the record do note that *Meet Molly* is the most expensive live show we produce . . ."

"Frank," Ben Warren broke in, "don't you at the same time get a better premium price than for any other program?"

"Of course, and you can see why when you look at the costs involved. Above the regular studio program costs—which I'll come back to in a minute—we average around $3,000 weekly in remote set-up charges and taping. Extra talent costs when she takes the music group out with her run another thousand a week *above* normal studio performance.

"But let's go back to the basic cost of the show. Molly gets $1,100 a week at present, and Harvey another 100 bucks for each of his guest news expert appearances. Molly gets a bonus of $25.00 for each spot run in the show.

"All of this adds up to the fact that the Heatherstones are drawing off slightly more than 50% of the total sales dollars! Her contract calls for all of this to go up about 8% for the next 52-week period. Can we raise the rate card to cover this?"

After a brief silence, White spoke: "I'll save our national sales guys from trying to answer that by offering some additional thoughts. From the talent point of view, Molly has one of the best contracts in the business—firm 52-week cycles, a four-week written notice of cancellation needed *or* an automatic renewal—and each renewal at an eight percent increase or better.

"How did we get into this position? This is a contract inherited from that brief period when Harry 'Escalator' Small was sent out from the home office to be controller. Harry had his station experience in an era of expansion, when it seemed that the rising curve of income and of TV household and market growth had no forseeable end.

"Harry put a carrot on a stick, in his thinking, and it's turned out that Molly ate the carrot and owns most of the stick!"

Summing up Molly

The final Molly decision must be White's: in the free exchange of his staff meeting, he has a divided house. Both his national sales manager and his New York sales representative are more than content to stand pat with a currently saleable product; his local sales manager, on the other hand, is unable to do much with Molly because of both price and attitude, and presumably would welcome a more economical program in which his staff could sell advertising for local clients. To drop the program would undoubtedly result in loss of national spot business, at least for a short period of time; a cheaper product would possibly bring in some local (but smaller) revenue.

The long-range projection, as detailed by May, Frank and Maurie, is less bright—points to additional cost, less net revenue, a static and aging audience. Even Warren admitted to an occasional stiffening among New York buyers. Could the program substantiate a rate increase without additional stiffening?

Top administration of the station group was fully aware of cost increases, and would make no complaints as long as revenue was proportionate *and* a dominant position was maintained, not only for the next 12-month cycle but for years beyond.

> THE CASE STUDY PROBLEM: As Jim White, write for group station management a firm recommendation and plan of action on *Meet Molly,* including whatever available documentation and opinion seems necessary to backstop a full and definitive decision.

SUGGESTED READINGS

(4) deSola Pool and Schramm — chapter 6 ("The Audience").

(12) Quaal and Brown — chapter 4 (see "Audience" references); chapter 5 (see "Costs of local programs").

(14) Roe — chapter 7 (see "Importance of time periods"), ("Counter-programming").

7

GOING ON THE AIR: A NEW 'U' IN VIEW

The Background

Duke Industries has built and put into successful operation three UHF TV stations in the past 12 years. Each of these is in a major market—none lower than 15th nationally—and each competes with at least four VHF commercial outlets.

Now Duke has received its construction permit and gone into the building of another UHF station, also in a major market *but* one that has been "under video-serviced" in the words of group vice president B. T. Wood.

Wood explains his point: "This has been a three-station market since the early 1950's—three substantial VHF stations, each with a longtime network affiliation, each with a standing in the community. An early, and in my mind premature, attempt to introduce a UHF operation died in bankruptcy—under-capitalized, programmed without experience, entered into at a time when too few home sets had the capacity to receive the UHF signal."

Wood's comments were offered before the management group assigned to put Channel 38 on the air. Mac Everett, the new general manager, had been station manager of Duke's first station, and the other team members had all worked in the Duke chain. "You've all," Wood continued, "had extensive and fiercely competitive experience under the gun in establishing one or more of our other stations. And it's because of that experience and that success you're here.

"But in some way this is a new ball game for all of us. In our three present markets, we came up against at least four VHF stations, plus VHF educational stations in two of the markets and a UHF competitor already established in one. There's a lot of programming that your new audience has never seen; also, you have a lot of material available that has never been purchased for play here due to lack of time to put it on.

"You have a number of ways to go. I'll be back in four weeks, and at that time I'd like to see a fairly comprehensive plan for programming, for promotion, for selling. Remember, our targeted air date is only three months away!"

THE PROBLEM

Everett and his staff faced an assignment that was both tough *and* a broadcaster's dream: literally to put a station on the air, covering every aspect of operation, with good financial backing and budgets, and the potential of an audience for new faces and new programs.

Mac Everett's first instruction to the group was obvious: "Split up, pull together everything in your own area, and next Monday we start a marathon meeting to put the jigsaw together."

Everett held preliminary individual conferences with each of the department heads: Brad Holloway, general sales manager; Jack Swope, program director; Farley James, news and sports director; Helen Masters, public affairs director; George Hansford, business manager; and Joey Haines, promotion manager. Without making judgments, he aided them in lining up reports on their respective areas.

The Planning Meeting

Everett opened the meeting by noting that the chief engineer was excused—"Out under a transmitter with a soldering gun. He says that if we know what we're doing, he'll get it on the air!"

"Now let's get to the business at hand. Each of you has a primary responsibility in one area. At the same time, we all have had past experiences in other markets, many of them applicable here—so it's any and all ideas from anyone who has something to offer. What goes on the air comes first, so I'll turn the meeting over to Jack for a programming discussion . . ."

baseball and football especially—who could be built into studio shows of their own. And it would sell."

Everett looked to his general sales manager, Brad Holloway.

HOLLOWAY: "Diversified programming is fun, and I don't deny the promotional opportunity implied. But I have to think of what our national spot sales reps can do with it, as well as our local salesmen. I'm a little afraid of an overload of kiddy programming—it's possible to have three gold trophies, and all the under-12-year-olds in town in your audience, and still not be able to sell the shows.

"I'm even more afraid of becoming sports-oriented in a secondary sort of way—never actually carrying major league action, but working with the stuff all around it. We may end up merely enhancing our competition!

"The news-every-hour leaves me cold. We might find interest on the part of a local advertiser or two, but it just isn't a currently-acceptable and understood pattern for national spot advertising.

"All-in-all, I'd like to see much more emphasis on feature films and syndicated shows, with as much of our money as possible directed to the purchase of the best possible packages. The rest of it can fill in as the need indicates."

Everett turned to Helen Masters, public affairs director: "We've heard from the commercial mainstream—what can you give us from here?"

MASTERS: "Our competitors are quite complacent in their current public service activities. They do church service pickups, run schedules of public service announcements for various local and national campaigns, and cooperate with the religious and civic organizations in the community.

"We have the opportunity to do something *different*. The weekday 9 a.m.-to-noon period can't possibly be very profitable. I suggest that we offer to the public and parochial schools the use of the time, to relay educational materials from National Educational Television and other sources—things they are not now receiving.

"There are weekend possibilities as well. We have the flexibility to air materials from the major religious groups—*not* in the early Saturday and Sunday morning 'ghetto' periods, but at afternoon times when the audience potential is much larger."

Everett turned to business manager George Hansford: "You've

not only been in the business a long time, but gone through the on-the-air pangs of two Duke stations. Any observations?"

HANSFORD: "I warn you, I'll sound grumpy; maybe even sour. There was a time when we put a station on for limited late afternoon and early evening hours, with one engineering shift covering the broadcast day. But this you don't want—we must land on the public full-blown, competing with established operations.

"This means two shifts of technical personnel from the beginning, offering 14-to-15 hours of air time as a potential.

"Now that's basic, and inside the studio. Farley talked about remote sports coverage—going outside to pick up athletic events, either live or on tape. This ups your labor and production costs by a substantial degree, and should be borne in mind. Who pays? Can we make money on it?

"Brad Holloway talks about syndicated shows and feature films as a mainstay of operation. Again, these cost money, real money, and while we can acquire some of those properties at a lesser cost than can our big VHF competitors, we will still have to pay on the basis of being in a major market. Can we sell them?

"Jack Swope wants to pick up personalities for live shows. Again we face the talent costs, the special fees, the promotional expenditures involved in making effective use of live talent.

"It isn't my job to negate any of these ideas, but only to offer warnings about the costs inevitably connected with various methods of operation. Coming into this market, we don't have the yardstick for per-hour costs of being on the air that we'll have a year from now. And our parent organization will understand all costs and problems—as long as we remember that they were incorporated to make a profit in the long run, not to lose!"

Everett nodded to promotion manager Joey Haines: "Any comments?"

HAINES: "Promotion effort will of course have to be designed to follow and support the pattern of programming. We have an adequate budget—the direction in which we point it will be the question.

"When our first station went on the air, we slanted all of our efforts to its UHF channel identification as an entity—we didn't lean on personalities or specific programs. With billboards, and in newspaper ads and on bus cards and a lot of other visual media, we had four dice—all sixes—inside a TV screen, with the slogan *24 is your lucky number*. And it evidently worked.

"But for our second station we went another route, using radio spots and small newspaper ads to push the personalities hosting specific shows, and the syndicated features and movie titles, just for the day at hand. And that worked, too.

"So we can lean to one extreme or the other, or possibly come up with a mix of the two. The direction of the programming will give the answer."

EVERETT (concluding the meeting): "You've all given me your very best thinking, and I appreciate it. I'll be back to you individually with questions, mostly about costs. We don't really have any open conflict between departments, and I hope to put all of your reports together and come up with a winner. Whatever way it goes, you'll know soon."

THE CASE STUDY PROBLEM: As Mac Everett, assemble a comprehensive plan for group vice president Wood, to include an overall program schedule, a prognosis of sales potential, and an outline of promotional support philosophy.

SUGGESTED READINGS

(2)	Brown	— see "UHF" references.
(3)	Coleman	— chapter 9 (disregard dates; note percentages against probable color percentage penetration in market).
(9)	Lichty and Topping	— see "UHF" references.
(12)	Quaal and Brown	— see references under "UHF"; also chapter 7 ("Managing for profit").
(14)	Roe	— chapter 4 ("The independent station").
(16)	Stanley	— p. 96 ("Program content," etc.).

8

WHO IS THE NEXT GENERAL MANAGER?

The Situation

Fred Grant is general manager of the broadcast division of ACL Communications Ltd., an international corporation with diversified interests in newspaper, magazine and book publishing. The ACL broadcast subsidiary, ACL Radio-TV, was established by the parent organization in the early days of TV; grew from an initial investment in one radio and TV station combine to its present group of five properties—each a combination radio-TV operation, each a network affiliate, each successful in its local market.

Grant is a career person with ACL; has seen management service in field offices and with the headquarters operation in New York. His credits are numerous and varied, including guest speaker invitations and chairmanships of industry organizations; his contacts with broadcast industry leaders are personal and informal, and his knowledge of industry activities and futures is current and sound.

In his position Grant commands the respect of the vice president-general managers in charge of each of the ACL broadcast properties. More strictly speaking, he has this working situation in four out of five of the station units, because there is no manager for the *fifth*, and newest, station.

ACL management policy toward its individual broadcast units has been a "hands-off—service your market in your own way" type of attitude. In the four established radio-TV properties of ACL (10 years or more of ownership), senior vice presidents are in charge. Given wide latitude in management and industry involvement, they are known as senior citizens in commercial broadcasting—nationally and even internationally.

ACL's newest station, WAAA-TV (and WAAA radio), has been a member of the group for less than a year. The previous general manager was a stockholding member of the former ownership group, and quite happily departed for an early retirement with his capital gains.

The Problem

Fred Grant faced a major problem: to select as the new head of the WAAA stations a well-qualified manager, a person who could in a reasonable length of time claim a position comparable to the other four members of what might be termed the peer group—the ACL general managers.

Knowing that personnel assignments at any level have an element of trial and error, Grant wanted to take the time to make the best possible choice—to "minimize the T&E, to maximize the possibility of success."

Grant's immediate superior is Ralph Lake—one of three executive vice presidents of ACL, the board member who led the corporation into broadcast investments, and most recently the man responsible for the acquisition of the WAAA property. As a senior member of the corporate board, Lake carries direct responsibility for the activities of the broadcast division.

Fred Grant must transmit his recommendation—or recommendations—to Lake, with as much screening of personnel records and documentation of accomplishments as he can put together.

Grant decides that this is a promotion that can come from within the ACL broadcast division: after more than 15 years of broadcast activity, it would (1) seem obvious that a candidate for the position could be found within the group, and (2) it would be a demoralizing action to go outside for a new major management candidate.

In an informal talk, Lake agreed: "I go along wholeheartedly with your thought of bringing someone up out of our own staff. But this must be a person who meets some difficult-to-define job speci-

Who is the Next General Manager?

fications as well as the obvious ones—the things that the Navy calls 'Running a tight ship.'

"From the business side, he or she will face the same problems as the man who runs any local chain of retail stores—stocking merchandise the public wants, advertising its availability to them, maintaining good relations with the users of his wares.

It demands skill and judgment in selecting and promoting good people, and in keeping a high staff morale level, and keeping one eye on the profit-and-loss figures every day!

"But there's a second part, and this is where broadcasting is a little different from a hardware chain. We have enemies—several kinds and in varying degrees. There are the outright competitors—the newspaper and regional magazines and outdoor advertising people. These are easy to recognize—they sell against us, even as we sell against them.

"The second group isn't hard to understand either. These are the editorial people of the print media, who look to and point to the shortcomings and mistakes of our industry with shouts of alarm.

"And we mustn't overlook those people, sincere and otherwise, who view our entire industry as a major contributor to everything from juvenile delinquency to inadequacies in Medicare!

"This is a rambling way of saying that the manager has to be quick, unflappable, skilled in public verbal fencing, and have the ability to keep a smile through it all!"

To a Solution

To meet the problem, Grant called for a meeting of his four senior station managers. In a lengthy, informal and confidential memo, he reviewed his conference with Lake, and concluded: "I don't like to sound arbitrary, but just for openers I want each of you to come up with a person, maybe two, from your own staff, who is the most likely candidate for the job. *Don't* discuss it with them; *don't* ask them if they want to move. I'll worry about that when we get to the finals.

"And don't hold back on me. Remember that this is for the good of the entire group—anybody who is *ready* isn't going to stay with us anyway, *if* they're that good. So even though it might hurt your own operation at this time, give me the best you have and we'll go from there."

The Meeting

Three weeks later Grant had his meeting with the four managers. Six names were submitted: two from each of two stations, one each from the other two. To Grant there were a few surprises in the list. In the general organizational structure, there was a station manager for each of the radio and TV stations; under each of these a national and a local sales manager, as well as a program manager.

Yet in several cases the general managers had omitted their number one people—the obvious successors to themselves.

"Why not Beardsley, your TV station manager?" Grant asked the head of ACL's oldest and best-known operation.

"Beardsley is a great representative for us and for the entire group," the veepee replied. "He's an officer of the Quad-A advertising group, a guest speaker for at least 20 industry groups each year, and a worker in a lot of other associations. Next year he'll be president of the NBR. He has contacts all over the broadcast field—but he's just not close enough to the day-by-day operation of our stations to supervise one.

"I'm giving you King as my first choice," the veepee continued. "He's doing a great job as national sales manager. Came up from radio production, back in our first year, and he's had a dozen different desks—traffic and production and local sales. Nice guy, and a nice family—fit in anywhere—and very down-to-earth with the staff. You put him out there, and you won't have any problems with personnel or in community relations."

Grant noted the King recommendation; at the same time put Beardsley's name in a parallel column, under a question mark.

From the second ACL manager Grant drew a more expected recommendation. "Wally Brown is doing an excellent job as TV station manager, and I'd hate to lose him. He started with us in TV as a staff announcer. He did news and weather shows; later became production manager and then program manager. He has a fine command of film buying and syndicated show buying as well. He supervises the publicity and audience promotion work. When our last national sales manager left us, we promoted him over several people with a lot of sales experience, because we thought that he could do the best job of representing us to our sales rep and to national clients. And from that it was a natural step to his present job as TV station manager."

"What about Granger?" Grant asked.

"He would be my second nomination. He's radio manager, and a very good one—a former career Army officer who came to us to do personnel work and gradually took on a lot of other duties. But only after we've talked about King."

Grant turned to his next manager.

"Ted Philipps is the best peddler any of us will ever see," the manager said, "and I wouldn't even mention his name if he hadn't trained a lot of good men under him.

"Phillips came to us from a used car lot. He made better money than we could offer him, but he was bored with the seasonal aspects of that kind of work. He went out as our newest local radio salesman, with the poorest sales prospect list on the staff: in a year, he was top biller, and a year later he was the top TV salesman on the staff. He became local radio sales manager, and then local TV sales manager, and now he is national sales manager for both stations. He knows all the timebuyers in New York and Chicago, and has a fine relationship with our sales reps."

The fourth ACL general manager smiled as he spoke: "Lou Garcia is our radio station manager and my prime candidate. He joined us as bookkeeper in the accounting department. He took his CPA in night school, and went on to a night school degree in business administration. He became chief accountant, and then business manager. As a member of our executive group he has offered sound suggestions and guidelines for rate card pricings, for film buying, for equipment purchases and amortizations, that have given us an edge over our competition. He understands the *business* of broadcasting, if you will, like few people I know. There were a few noses out of joint when we made him station manager last year—but there is a lot of respect for his knowledge and ability as well. If we want to put one of our good career men out to run a station as *we* see it, you couldn't pick a better man. And I'll be sad to see him go."

"But suppose we looked at Fairbank?" Grant asked.

"I couldn't argue," the veepee added. "Parker is a younger

man, came out of the executive training program, and has been with us in several positions, and done them all well. He has vigor, and a wide understanding of the broadcast business, and would most likely do a good job."

On his note pad Grant had the six names submitted—plus the personal side entry of Beardsley, his question mark notation from the first manager, and B. J. Blodgett, who as national sales manager of the ACL group reported directly to him.

"At this stage," he said, "we've assembled a wide range of good people. Unless any of you has very specific knowledge of why any of them would *not* move, I think we can stop without a go-around of second or third choices. Anybody?"

"Good choices—they'll go," was the conclusion of the group.

For Action

Following the management meeting, Grant put together a prospectus report for his meeting with Ralph Lake. He assembled *dossiers* on the top people proposed by his managers—plus his own nominations of Beardsley and Blodgett:

BROWN, WALLACE R. Station manager, WBBB-TV. Age 41; two years junior college, Chicago, one year special course in broadcast law, Howard U. Prior experience: local radio traffic clerk, staff announcer. Joined WBBB as staff announcer—news, weather, staff duties; subsequently production manager, program manager, station manager. Married, two children, active in church, P-TA, Rotary.

GARCIA, LOUIS J. Station manager, WCCC Radio. Age 42; Queens College, New York, three years; CPA, night school; bachelor in business administration, evening division, U. of C. Prior experience: bookkeeper. Joined WCCC accounting department; chief accountant, business manager, station manager. Married, four children, active in Knights of Columbus, local politics, broadcast associations.

GRANGER, MICHAEL T. Station manager, WBBB Radio, and regional Manager for CATV development. Age 51; West Point graduate, career Army officer, joined station as personnel manager after early retirement; later assumed business manager duties as well. Married, four children, national officer in veterans' organization, head of local former officers' group, active in politics.

FAIRBANK: PARKER L. National sales manager WCCC-TV. Age 35; prep school, Yale B.A. and Wharton School M.B.A. Trainee in ACL magazine division, transferred to broadcasting as local sales manager for WDDD Radio, then to WCCC as TV local sales manager; just promoted to present title. Married, two children; top-seeded player in amateur tennis; weekend sailor; active in local Yale Club recruitment.

KING, ROGER S. National sales manager, WDDD-TV. Age 43; B.A. in communications, U. of Illinois. Prior experience: announcer, program manager, Peoria, Ill. radio station. Joined WDDD staff as radio director; traffic manager, TV production, local TV sales, local sales manager. Married, three children; golfer; active in civic clubs, P-TA county council.

PHILLIPS, THEODORE A. National sales manager, WEEE and WEEE-TV. Age 37; no college. Prior experience: retail salesman. Joined station as local radio salesman; TV sales staff; local radio sales manager; local TV sales manager. Single, active in civic clubs, golfer, district delegate for Quad-A advertising convention, regional representative to NBR national convention of broadcasters.

. . . and Grant's appended suggestions. . . .

BEARDSLEY, REGINALD H. Station manager, WDDD-TV. Age 45; B.A. Williams College. Prior experience: local radio salesman, Salem, Mass., TV spot sales representative, Boston and New York. Joined ACL New York office as service executive; to WDDD as local TV sales manager, national sales manager. Married, three children; active in national industry groups, frequent speaker for industry meetings, for schools and for educational groups.

BLODGETT, B. J. National sales manager, ACL Communications Ltd. Group. Age 35; Pembroke B.A. and American University M.A. in American History. Prior experience: promotion assistant, *Time;* sales promotion manager, New York City FM station; local sales manager, NYC AM major station. Joined ACL group headquarters as advertising and promotion manager before promotion to present position. Active as officer in New York chapter of American Women in Radio and Television; adjunct professor at city college. Single (divorced); most recently delegate to NOW convention.

> THE CASE STUDY PROBLEM: As Fred Grant, make a number one selection for the position, and for a meeting with Ralph Lake prepare a full line of reasoning for this choice. At the same time, be prepared with a number two selection, with similar reasons.

SUGGESTED READINGS

(6) Emery — see references under "Management responsibilities."
(12) Quaal and Brown — chapters 1, 2, 3, 7, 9 are of special relevance, as is the text generally by the implication of its title.
(14) Roe — chapters 1 and 3.

9

THE COST OF BEING INDEPENDENT

An Immediate Problem Situation

Ben Charleton called his department heads together for an emergency meeting, and opened without preliminary chatter: "Gentlemen, I will confirm for you the rumor that you already know—we have lost our network affiliation, and 75 days from today will be an independent station, responsible for our own programming from sign-on to sign-off!"

The Background

The situation was serious, but not entirely unexpected. Charleton's Channel 11, along with the present independent station, Channel 8, had entered the Tri-Cities market in the mid-1950s —both latecomers in comparison to Channels 2 and 5, early 1949 pioneers in the area. The combination of a late start and a high band placement (from the common antenna tower in the downtown area, 8 and 11 simply couldn't reach as far as the low band stations) made 8 an economy-minded, tightly-run operation, airing its abbreviated daily schedule "on the cheap," in the words of a local TV critic.

And 11 was only slightly better; a very weak network affiliate, even for the recognized number three network. Junie Barthold, head of station relations for that network, sent continuing crisp reminders and jabs to Charleton, reminding him of 11's relative standing in the local market *and* in its performance as contrasted with other network affiliates in similar markets. "Congratulations," he wired, "you are now number 29 out of 30 in the Nielsen MNA report. Why not try for 30?"

Charleton had made obvious tries to climb out of the bottom category, but found many problems. Lack of signal strength was a major factor: the Tri-Cities, as a mecca for a five-state area from the mid-1800's, was ringed by communities of 20- to 30,000 persons, all just one day's stagecoach ride removed from the market center, and all within the signal of Channels 2 and 5 but far enough removed to pick up a fuzzy, "snowy" image from Channel 11.

And the population of these onetime crossroads hamlets totaled, when swung around all compass points, over 300,000—a potential advantage in terms of *total viewers reached* that was impossible to combat.

The rapid growth of CATV was some small help as reflected in outside audience reports, but not enough to overcome the entrenched strength of the dominent TV signals.

A pioneer VHF educational station, funded by the state university and a number of small colleges, sometimes intruded in the audience potential with films from the BBC.

A private investor's UHF experiment had tried for 18 months, and gone out of business.

The potential for a VHF "drop-in" was being explored by the Federal Communications Commission.

Where does Charleton look next?

The Channel 11 Image

The "image" of his Johnny-come-lately station was another problem to Charleton: in this basically conservative area many people, and especially the older and more permanent residents, had been served by Channels 2 and 5 for six years before Channels 8 and 11 had begun even part-time operations. They had the *Today* and *Tonight* shows, and their favorite network personalities, as well as their always-watched news and weather and sports reporters, and saw little reason to tune to new fields where strangers peered back at them.

Also, lack of success forced economies in operation: Charleton had fewer newsmen and less mobile equipment, a smaller promotion staff and an even smaller budget for promoting his wares, than did his established competitors. He couldn't pay prime rates for feature films, or for syndicated kiddy shows and cartoons. While he strained his budget to procure and to retain the best possible talent, he nevertheless lost good people to local competition and to larger markets.

Seeking a Solution

In the special meeting, Charleton had no need to review those facts at hand. "Channel 8 is getting the network affiliation. You know and I know that it's going to be close to impossible for them to do any better than we have done. At the same time I think we have to be objective enough to understand why the network is making the move—Barthold is a gambler, and he figures that something better might come out of the switch.

"And so much for that," Charleton continued. "Now *we* have a problem. We are going to re-program ourselves, be on the air more hours than 8 ever was, offer better features and production and client service and more comprehensive news coverage than they ever did, and be a fully competitive television service in this market. This is your challenge—*how* are we going to do it?"

"Right now, Ben?" the program manager asked.

As laughter broke the tension, Charleton replied: "No George, not today. Everybody go back to the troops and tell them what I've told you—I'll follow it with a memo. Tomorrow we'll meet for a quick exchange of thoughts, with the guarantee that no decisions will be made. In two weeks we'll meet to define our directions. Then we'll have 30 days to firm up our plans, and a final 30 days to promote and sell what we're going to do. I'll see you tomorrow."

Charleton opened the next day's meeting: "We've all had a night to sleep on, or *not* sleep on, the situation. Let's start with some questions."

The promotion manager spoke: "Ben, just for the record, how serious is this from a financial point of view? Couldn't we do just as well without those hours when we only get 30-something per cent value in network compensation?"

Charleton nodded to Joe White, his business manager: *"You can answer that."*

White shifted some papers. "Roughly, our real value—the selling price of the station, if you will—just went from about $11 million to $3½ million! Now that's a little severe, and it's in terms of what the network affiliation is worth *here,* at this moment in time, as opposed to what past performance has shown an independent to be worth in this market. Two years from now we might be able to demonstrate that an independent is worth $5 million or even $6 million."

"But not 11," the program manager sighed.

"No, not 11," White continued, "and here's why. At present, our annual income is forecast at about $2.8 million, from all sources, of which about $800,000 is network compensation. No pun intended, that's now a net loss.

"Another $1.2 million is in national spot business—of which we must note that about 65% is in network time, as station breaks in network time periods. And that's why network time is worth more than 30-something per cent of the rate card!"

"The remaining $800,000 is in local billing, with approximately 20% of this in network time periods."

"So," Charleton concluded, "without an adding machine, you can see that we will almost automatically lose a little over 50% of our income. How we hold, or recapture, the rest, is up to us."

"What kind of rate card will we have?" . . . "Do we pick up the syndicated programs that Channel Eight carries as an independent?" . . . "How about expanding kiddy shows in the afternoon?" . . . "How about a longer news program, maybe starting earlier?"

The questions flew, and Charleton noted them; after 10 minutes he held up his hand. "Okay, we've heard the basic financial situation, and we're thinking along those lines. Each of you has a well-defined area: national sales, local sales, programming, news, engineering, promotion, business management—and I'm *not* listing them in order of importance.

"By your questions you have indicated to one another as well as to me the direction of your thinking. Explore your own area, communicate with one another, check with me, as I'll be doing with you—and two weeks from today we'll meet to make plans."

The Planning Meeting

Charleton opened the scheduled meeting: "I have met with each of you, and in some cases with two or more people. We've reviewed, and re-reviewed, and compromised in some places and been firm in others. Let me offer a few introductory remarks: First of all, I'd like to take an optimistic note and sum up what we *have* going for us. We *are* established—we are not in the position of a new station entering the market, or in that of a UHF having to sell the basic concept of investment in antenna adjustment just to receive us.

"We have in the past drawn as much as 40% of the tune-in. This was of course with special network programming, which we no longer will carry—but the point is that with the right program appeal we have the physical ability to attract an audience on that order, and that is a point to remember well.

"We know our engineering limitations, and there is little that we can do about them. But we should remember that Channel Eight has almost the same problems and the same acceptance problems in this community situation.

"For the first year, I think it would be foolish for us to consider ourselves in competition with either Two or Five. Between them they will command 60% to 65% of the audience, and the same ratio of dollars in national spot revenue. Beyond that it's an open road, and I propose to get the lion's share of the remaining audience and dollars! I would guess that the working theme is 'Beat Eight,' and how we go about that is today's real topic."

"I don't like it, Ben," national sales manager Bart Houston said. "When our sales reps in New York or the other big cities go out to submit availabilities, they're in competition with the reps from all three stations, not just one. We *have* to keep an eye on all the others."

"Keeping an eye on 'em is okay, but the real dollar value competition comes down to us and Eight," local sales manager Larry Barth added. "Here at the local level we've never been in serious competition with the big boys—but with Eight we can put up a fight—and usually a winning one."

Joe White: "From the business office point of view, how we

structure our rates will help us define a lot of this. Do we stand firm; drop to expected low levels, or what?"

"Stand firm," Houston replied. *"But* shift the programming to a feature movie concept, with minute-or-larger availabilities throughout the day. Then we can package groups of spots shotgunned to reach a lot of people in a week, or even in a broadcast day. We can commission a rating outfit to document reach and frequency, and sell a lot."

"No, we can't go that route, unless we want to lose a lot of local clients who have identification with a certain program or personality. We'll have to pull our rates back until we see what kind of audience we draw, just to keep the people we have now." Larry Barth continued: "There are local programs where this idea of pouring in spots would change the whole attitude of the present sponsors."

Charleton turned to George Turner, his program manager: "You have at least a few words on this?"

"At least," George replied. "I think you guys both have a point, up to a certain extent—also that you are holding too fast to an easy out in terms of past clients locally or in the current performance of our chums at Eight with the movie grind. If we want to create some excitement—to gamble on the attraction of something new—then we are going to have to compromise and make a really new kind of format.

"We didn't lose our license; just our network feed. Financially this hurts. There are prime time periods when I think it would be foolish to run up against network programming—we'd only be denting our pick on a granite wall.

"In other times we have to find weaknesses, and attack these with the best materials we can pull together. The fact that the total daytime audience rarely goes over 30% of the potential, and even the prime time sits at about 60%, gives us a challenge to do something that will bring *new* audience as well as pull existing audience from the competition."

"A nice sentiment," Houston said, "but how do you do it?"

"I'll try this on you for size," Turner replied, opening a large chart. "Here's the plan in a very rough Monday-Friday form . . ."

"You might very well want some explanation," Turner continued.

CHANNEL 11 MONDAY-THROUGH-FRIDAY PROGRAM SCHEDULE

8:45 a.m. sign-on; miscellany

9:00 a.m. to 11:00 a.m.	light variety, with a morning host; alternating between 30-minute syndicated shows and feature films, on a random basis.
11:00 a.m. to 12:00 noon	*Ourtown Spotlight:* a live hour, with host and possibly hostess; interviews, film shorts, news and weather information, entertainment.
12:00 noon to 1:00 p.m.	A kiddy hour: An "Uncle Louie" type host; cartoon features; opportunity for live commercials by host.
1:00 p.m. to 4:00 p.m.	*Double Feature Matinee:* two back-to-back short features, with repeats on a four-to-six week cycle. Live host an optional feature for commercials.
4:00 p.m. to 7:00 p.m.	Solid kiddy shows; a pot pourrie of everything available, both in cartoon and human-action format; tape commercials by Uncle Louie from earlier period.
7:00 p.m. to 7:30 p.m.	*Ourtown Evening Spotlight:* feature news, accent on local interviews and happenings, including top-of-the-news national and international happenings, weather, etc.
7:30 p.m. to 9:30 p.m.	* Action-adventure-western syndicated programs, in a random pattern of 30-60 minute lengths.
9:30 p.m. to 10:30 p.m.	*Ourtown Tonight:* news and features, including taped interviews and features from earlier segments; weather, sports results, etc. Top host in charge.
10:30 p.m. to sign-off	feature movie (or syndicated interview show, if available).

"Or an explanation of how we sell it," Barth grumbled.

"Okay—here we go. First of all, it would be foolish to turn the station on and bring in crew for the early morning—we have nothing competitive to offer. At least until we are in a stronger position.

"From 9 to 11, we are up against all kinds of quiz shows and network reruns of situation comedies—I suggest a personable host with a bag of variety programs, all the way from silent shorts to full-length old movies. This is a fun time; the kids have gone off to school, the man of the house to work, and it's for relaxing.

"Along about 11, we need a better focus on the day. Here we have a hostess and probably a secondary host as well—service information, everything locally oriented, with our news and weather guys coming in as needed.

"Noon is for the kids—over 80% of the local school kids in the elementary grades go home for lunch, and we go for them here with cartoons and a nice, lovable host.

"At 1 p.m. they're out again, and we now offer some relaxation for the lady of the house. These will be familiar films, and will come back again fast—the purpose is to gain a large cumulative audience over a period of time. It's the place they'll look to see if they want today's offering.

"From 4 p.m. all the way to 7, I want to capture the kiddy audience. We know that they are available, and I want to give them what they want. We scale this from the youngest interest early in the three-hour block to older interests in the last half-hour. In no way do we attempt to compete with the news programming on the other channels.

"At 7, when the other guys have turned to filling in until the network starts, we do a capsule review of the day—a combination news and program production.

"From 7:30 to 9:30 we run all over the place with action-type shows, not at any time trying to counter-program any single slot against one or more network programs. We have a lot of leeway here in experimenting in best formulas, and I'll admit that this might develop into a firmer schedule than you see at the moment.

"At 9:30 we jump the gun by 30 minutes with the start of a full hour of news and features. We feed heavily on tapes of earlier local segments; also drop in evening news and late-developing items.

"10:30 to closing is our most open time. While movies have proven to be the best overall vehicles against network personality shows, we must stay open for a new personality in syndication if anything pops up.

"Overriding the evening schedule at any time would be the possibility of sports feeds, as indicated. We should be open to anything—even soccer, if it suddenly takes hold!

"Now," Turner grinned at both Turner and Barth, "before you see too many problems in selling at both the national and local levels, let me point this out—spot participations are available here through most of the day. At the same time, the local sponsor who needs identification can buy the weatherman with his inserts at *several times* during the day, or the news guy he fancies, or the lady hostess of the morning show. We should be able to balance this so that both sides are happy."

Charleton turned to his staff: "And there's a plan to think about. I don't want George to stand and defend every detail, but I'd like your responses as they come to mind . . ."

Houston spoke first: "There's lots there from a national sales viewpoint—for the most part I like it, and I think our reps will. But three hours of kiddy stuff in a solid block is an awful lot—I wonder if we shouldn't stay with our present news at 6 p.m. and see what happens."

News director Paul Petersen was dissatisfied: "This gives short shrift to news as real *news*—we end up as sort of second-rate contributors to some programs, but don't have any real identity."

Barth was next: "My reservations run along Paul's line of thinking. I don't know how we sell a news show unless it is labeled as a news show, and scheduled and promoted that way. I see what George means in floating features through an hour or half-hour, but I don't know how we sell that concept. News is news, and weather is weather, and sports is sports, and the other stations will continue to offer that kind of identity and advertising opportunity."

Petersen added: "I hate to see us give up the morning. We've been doing a 15-minute news for almost seven years, and while I admit it doesn't show up in the ratings, it's part of our image."

"That nighttime sports thing scares me," Houston said. "If we get a client sold on the audience turnover in the evening, and then bump him because of a hockey game, we'll have trouble in the future."

"I'd like to see us retain every bit of identity we now have," Barth said. "We should try to hold our present audience where we can, not toss it out along with the loss of the net. My salesmen will fight to keep clients where they are now, even if it means reducing our rate card to compensate."

"Well," Charleton concluded, "we've got some pretty clear-cut opinions and attitudes. George and I have the onus on us to come up with an initial program plan—the immediate following step will be a practical sales plan to go along with it. So much for today."

THE CASE STUDY PROBLEM: As Ben Charleton, establish a firm program format for the "new, independent Channel 11," using whatever staff opinions seem valid to you plus whatever additional opinion and information you have at your command. An explanation for the action should accompany all major decisions.

SUGGESTED READINGS

(9) Roe — chapter 4 ("The independent station"); chapter 7 ("Programming for the commercial station"); chapter 14 ("Sales management for the independent").

(12) Quaal and Brown — Various readings under headings of sales, programming, management, etc. There is no specific reference to the independent station as such; however, co-author Quaal wrote from a background as head of WGN-TV Chicago, one of the country's leading independents.

10

WHAT DID HE/SHE SAY?

To the mouse, cheese is cheese—that's why mousetraps work
Wendell Johnson

This scribbler was writing a series of radio spots highlighting the contributions of church leaders during the Revolutionary War —a bicentennial stunt, of course. Of Peter Muhlenberg, a Lutheran preacher who stepped from his pulpit to take command of a colonial regiment and rose to major general, then became a leader in the early congress, I said: "Clergyman, warrior, statesman, an early distinguished citizen . . ."

The editing policy came back: We no longer use *man* in these forms; it's *person*. And while *warrior* isn't on the delete list it has a male superiority connotation.

Now I was not about to write "Clergyperson, army person, statesperson"! So in much wordier form I compromised with: "From the pulpit, on the battlefield, in the halls of congress, an early . . ." A neat save, and almost poetic—but it cost me 11 words instead of three, and knocked out another line in the 60-second spot.

NBC's Edwin Newman posed the question, "Will America be the death of English?" in his penetrating book, *Strictly Speaking*. (His prognosis: yes.) Newman assembled his text at a particularly fortituous time, when he had all of the Watergate language available plus the Monday night hyperbole of Howard Cossell and Alex Karras. If he had done nothing but reprint alternating chapters of press conferences and football commentary it would have been a notable service; with his commentary *Strictly Speaking* is a "must" for communicators.

Broadcasters can do little about dictionary-spouting press secretaries or redundant senators; and perhaps this is to the good. Television, by simply putting its cameras and microphones in the Army-McCarthy hearings of the early 1950's, may have done its most significant service ever to the public.

But, as more and more athletes move from the gridiron and the diamond up to the broadcast booth, we stand in danger of trading clarity for celebrity name value. Professional guards and shortstops understand fines: possibly a language control device might be a monitoring system that deducted $50 for each use of "You win 'em one at a time," $100 for "That's the name of the game," $250 for "He done pretty good," and $500 for "This is a team that come to play ball." But, according to Newman, there wouldn't be any conversation left!

Right on, man! Which is to return to the point. Sexism in the spoken and written language faces everyone in communications. Nowhere is the subject of greater sensitivity than in broadcasting, where the ascertainment of adequate, even superadequate, attention to those venerable "public interest, convenience and necessity" standards of the Federal Communications Commission becomes increasingly important. Feminist groups, keenly attuned to the insult in radio and TV language, stand ready to join forces with all other groups seeking station licenses; even look to making claims on their own.

One veteran news director said it candidly: "First it was *Ms*. Now I don't care if our press relations department has to make some changes in Addressograph plates because the female columnists won't accept a mailing sent to *Miss* or *Mrs*. But what does *Mizz* sound like on the air? Ten years ago, had one of my people voiced *Mizz* in a report, I would have fired the guy for making Coretta King sound like a laundress in Hattiesburg, Mississippi. Are we to replay *Showboat* in the cause of women's lib?"

What Did He/She Say?

Comes next the *person* gambit. As our societal structure becomes a bit more enlightened the thrust of the female contribution emerges—as of course it should, if only in homage to those late 19th and early 20th century ladies who pushed forward despite the "Pray to God, she will take care of you" jokes and all the rest of the harrassment. But we face a key word: *Chairman.*

No, not chairman—chair*person!* The VND (Veteran News Director) comes back: "For how many years, at all levels of government and in all kinds of public and private groups, from the P-TA and the VFW to the ACLU, have we reported on the statements of or the election of the *chairman?* We will accept the wording of press releases; we will accept 'new' terminology—but I wonder about the public. *Chairperson* to me is an awkward word —if I had my way I'd make it completely honest and say *chairwoman* when the post was female. This would underscore the point that a capable woman occupied the chair."

Some of us, when we read in an enlightened newspaper that "Everts bumped Casals in three hard-fought sets," wondered at what that revered violoncelle virtuoso had had happen to him; the realization that they meant two female tennis stars, Rosie Casals and Crissy Everts, came a moment later.

From other guidelines we are told that *forefathers, founding fathers, brotherhood, manpower, manmade,* all are no-noes: *ancestors, founders, companionship, human power, manufactured,* will substitute quite adequately.

The concept of "the common man" is now that of *the average citizen,* while "The family of man" is *the human family.*

There is no longer an *American Indian,* or a descendent thereof: only "native Americans"—which may well deny other historical concepts of what happened on our continent in eons past.

Is There a Definition?

For many working in ethical journalism, the New York *Times Manual of Style and Usage* is a convenient and authoritative guide. Its fourth printing, in late 1976, was keyed on for what it would say about *Ms.* "MS (two caps) is defined as representing *manuscript; Ms.* (cap *M* and small *s*) is called an 'honorific, use it only in quoted matter, in letters to the editor and, in news articles, in passages discussing the term itself.' "

(Readings in various categories in that text are cited below; indicated here as mandatory to the case study.)

> THE CASE STUDY PROBLEM: The newsroom and the public affairs department of the local broadcast operation will receive an increasing flow of communications, press releases and tapes that will reflect these semantic problems. Much will come to the management desk for resolution.
>
> How to work with them, how to establish a viable and defensible policy, is the subject.

SUGGESTED READINGS

(8) Jordan — in addition to "Ms.," see readings and cross-references under "male, female, man, woman, women's liberation, NOW," etc.

(11) Newman — look for most of above references; also note section on sports reporting on the air.

(13) Rivers — see "Guidelines for newswriting about women"; also parts of AP-UPI Stylebook.

PART II

Case Study Profiles

Profile 1

THE BUSINESS MANAGER'S PROBLEM: RETOOLING FOR ENG

WAAA-TV news director Jow Brown attended both the annual meetings of the Radio-Television News Directors Association and the National Association of Broadcasters. The displays of new electronic video equipment, and the tales of great successes in almost-instantaneous news beats, had his juices running high: he wanted it—all of it—and he wanted it right away.

WAAA-TV, in a half-million household market, had enjoyed a number one news position in ratings for at least 10 years; no serious challenge has held for more than a month or two, and the present position continued to be strong.

But Joe saw a dim future unless his sizeable news operation was re-equipped with a considerable array of the hardware called ENG—Electronic News-Gathering Equipment—*and soon*.

In his ebullient concept of a bright new world, at a staff meeting before general manager George Jolliffe, Joe faced the sharp accountant's pencil and below-the-line reasoning of business manager Mel Berkson. A seasoned financial officer of the group-owned WAAA-TV, Berkson was accountable not only to his own general manager but to the group financial vice-president.

"Immediacy" was the key word in Joe's presentation. "Lightweight cameras, one-inch tape economy, fast tape editing, beating the competition," all followed.

"And of course," he added, "the potential for economical production of on-site commercials with this equipment is an added plus."

Berkson sighed: "I recall some early days, when we had limited 16mm. film equipment, for news but supposedly available for local commercial production. But when a fire broke out at First and Main, we left the sponsor hanging with his talent costs and ran off to the fire!"

"Simple," Joe answered. "We must have enough portable equipment to answer both needs."

Manager Jolliffe looked to his business manager: "Mel, how does that stack up in terms of dollars—real dollars—in terms of capital investment and depreciation?"

"Not very well," Berkson answered. "On a 10-year write-off of investment in film hardware—cameras, editing units, support hardware—we have justified about 20 per cent this year, and can go for about 10 per cent each year after this, tapering off in five-to-six years. The most expensive unit—the film processing section—has seven years to go.

"Our news, in both evening periods, has been profitable for us—modestly so, but always healthy on the black side of the ledger—for the past 10 years. We certainly want to maintain the dominant position that will continue that kind of budget history. But the type of hardware investment that Joe suggests, on the order of $500,000 in an 18-month period, would put that budget line into a decidedly red position. And what do we do with this unwritten-off film hardware—sell it as boat anchors?"

Program manager Mort Swanson spoke: "As far as the public is concerned, it doesn't make much difference whether we use tape or film. The audience isn't interested in the difference, unless it's truly live. They aren't gaining anything if a story is put on by tape just to demonstrate that kind of capability. That might end up a promotional gimmick, and the public gets bored after a while. They've seen a "moon walk" live, and international satellite transmission and all the rest. Big deal. Why bring in a feature story "live"—meaning wobbly hand-held tape cameras—when it could be done better on film?

"We can be originating from a tin shack, or the fanciest studios in town," Swanson continued, "but what we offer the viewer —*through the tube*—is what matters. "The techniques, and the film or electronic gear involved, are up to us. We do what we can afford to do."

Suggested Discussion Points:

- Is ENG so dominant and compelling a way to go that present film equipment should be scuttled?
- Can existing film equipment and modest investments in ENG operation be balanced?
- Is it possible to maintain a dominant film operation?

SUGGESTED READINGS

(12) Quaal and Brown — parts of chaps. 7 and 8.
(14) Roe — references under "financial management" and "engineering."

Also, this is a subject where researching issues of *Broadcasting* and *Television/Radio Age* in the March-April periods of annual NAB meetings would be useful.

Profile 2

COOKING A LEGAL STEW

A cautionary note: this is a painfully true case study of the problems of the station manager of a major market network-owned outlet in the ancient pre-television days of radio supremacy.

If you think that similar legal problems haven't happened, or can't happen, in TV or CTAV or whatever the medium—*move on to the next case study.*

But if some nagging doubt causes you to think that history can and does repeat itself, simply multiply all of the figures by five and contemplate the consequences for you, the station manager!

Waldo Partridge Starrs (his professional name) had conducted an extremely popular cooking show on WAAA Radio for almost seven years. He was an egotistical and temperamental performer, proud of his *cordon bleu* credentials and of his program subtitle and introduction: "The Kitchen Conjuror."

With a rich baritone voice tinged by just a bit of a mysterious, *mittel*-European accent, plus a solid knowledge of food preparation, Starrs was a sold-out item on the station log.

Unfortunately, television was as damaging to daytime radio cooking programs as to nighttime dramatic and musical fare. The time came when advertising dollars were no longer available for a kind of programming that had now gone visual: Waldo was cancelled at the end of his contract period.

This was a major blow to Starrs. His expertise was in radio communications: the ability to talk about foods and food service amenities in a sophisticated way—*galantine* of turkey and holiday table decorations, Yorkshire pudding and *Viennertorte,* Pennsyl-

this: over the seven year period he figures that about 1.8 million recipes were sent out—and that's from WAAA promotion claims, remember. And he's willing to round off his rights for a flat 10 cents apiece!

"Then there are the client use and magazine printings and whatnot. For these plus the mailings he'll settle for a flat $250,000, without argument."

Carruthers sighed: "That's highway robbery. But you're the legal counsel—can he do it?"

Reynolds nodded: "The problem is that we don't have a shred of evidence to show that he ever agreed to it, or was compensated for the material as a part of his contract. It was standard promotional activity, sure, but try to prove it. He can drag into court literally wheelbarrow loads of *our* mastheads, and say, 'I never got a penny for this—I was exploited.' And we can come up with a lot of arguments, but he is going to be established as the damaged and now cast-off former employee."

"Okay, Hal, what do we do?"

"Two things," Reynolds replied. "First of all, we settle with Waldo for $100,000—this is what I believe he and his brother-in-law need to open 'Waldo's Conjuror's Kitchen' in Berwyn—which is what they want. And as a bonus we grant them the use of the show title—which we happen to own! And we write it off to experience."

"I agree," Carruthers answered. "But what's point two?"

"You have a staff meeting as soon as possible, and re-examine your practices with other shows and other performers, and figure out some iron-clad ways to keep this from happening again!"

Suggested Discussion Points

Waldo said on his program that the recipes *were* available; on the strength of this, should the threatened suit have been allowed to come into court, and opposed?

Could WAAA management have anticipated the Waldo vs. WAAA claims from an early date, and made an agreement that would have avoided the potentially-explosive situation?

In the future, how can WAAA management cover similar situations with adequate agreements between performers and management? Should similar agreements then be applied to writers, directors, producers, involved in potentially-exploitable productions?

SUGGESTED READINGS

(6) Emery — see "performing contracts," etc.
(12) Quaal & Brown — see "need for legal counsel."
(19) Zuckman & Gaynes — see "contracts"; "union and guild assignments," etc.

Profile 3

MUST IT BE "EDITORIALIZE OR PERISH"?

The problems of Station WBBB-TV, as they relate to the subject of "editorializing" on the air, are summed up in the following memorandum from the general manager to the group vice president:

As you know, I have for a long time resisted the concept of WBBB's taking stands on issues, of grinding the axe of partisan points of view; in short, of editorializing on the air.

This is as we recognize in the tradition of print journalism. There is scarcely a weekly paper published in the smallest of county seats that doesn't have an editorial column or more, calling for more support for the Boy Scouts or less speeding on the local stretch of the thruway or for a solution to the inchworm plague in the next county. Distant issues have roles as well: let's have a local rally to end a civil war in Africa, or what a shame it is that the old luxury trains of yesteryear no longer serve us.

None of these subjects has any relevant quality in terms of the overall community as defined by our signal; *and* we are licensed to serve this community—or so it says in the Federal Communications Act.

In the recent past, I've seen what has happened when one of our two competitors moved to editorialize. Station "A" put both light and heat on the local public utility, with films documenting the statement that the utility's stacks were pouring polluted air on the downtown and adjacent suburban news. The utility cancelled its sponsorship of the 10 o'clock news—immediately.

Station "B" fell into the same air pollution trap a little later, with a series of interviews with and statements by authorities to show a significant air pollution increase in the downtown area—because more and more private cars were being driven into the city.

The regional car dealers' associations all cancelled their schedules, as did the operator of the largest department store—the one with the brand-new 800-car parking ramp!

Under pressure from church groups, Station "A" started a campaign for the closing of all retail stores on Sunday. The three major food chains all withdrew their advertising.

Station "B" undertood to aid the cause of the regional Parent-Teacher Association in de-emphasizing competitive sports among junior high and grade school youngsters. The big sporting goods store cancelled its spot advertising, and an executive whose brother was head of the city park system sports program also withdrew the advertising of his corporation.

But I've also noted the continuing urge of our news director and of our public affairs manager to editorialize. We've all seen and heard the messages from members of the FCC, our own National Association of Broadcasters and other industry groups, to get in there and fight. Then we saw the sobering words of an FCC examiner in turning down the license renewal request of a west coast station: that one of the most serious points against the station was that it had a firm policy *not* to editorialize. This, he emphasized, made them suspect, and certainly guilty of not servicing their community.

So now we *have* editorialized. We did it graphically, pictorially, with film and candid photos as well as with words. We did it with concealed tap recorders and anonymous interviews; with checking and re-checking of facts and figures; with the best available staff and most of all with a sense of responsibility.

We took as our subject the most fundamental issue we could offer the public we are licensed to serve—*our* city, Everytown. We filmed the morning and evening traffic jams; all-day parking in no parking zones; industrial waste pouring into the river; women soliciting in broad daylight in the downtown area; bars open way after legal closing hours; piles of refuse and dirty public parks and policemen sleeping in patrol cars.

What happened? First of all we lost five clients, who cancelled abruptly because of "changes in advertising strategy." They all showed up on another station the next week.

Now we are told that the city itself is considering a lawsuit—because we have damaged its ability to get the best possible rates on a new bond issue; are told that we will be considered liable for the difference in rates between the anticipated one and what they might have to accept because of our slurs upon the character of and operation of the municipal administration.

And, following this, we are told that individual members of that administration may then file suits, based on defamation of character as implied by our revelations of their lack of or shoddy administration.

We think we can meet all of this heads-on, if we have to; but our job is broadcasting, not functioning in courts of law—and especially so when our cameras and microphones are still not admitted in those courts.

They say that in the academic world the unwritten law is "publish or perish." From recent governmental dictat, we would infer that our command is "editorialize or perish" (meaning lose your license).

But if it then in truth becomes the reality of "editorialize *and* perish," who's the winner?

Suggested Discussion Points

Are there "safe" areas of subject matter that a station can use while fulfilling its implied requirement to editorialize?

Should a station follow a policy, as is common with print media, of endorsing political candidates?

In the same way, should a station take sides on controversial issues in its community: school expansion, bond issues, rezoning of land and buildings, police action, etc.?

Is there any way in which a station can follow an aggressive policy of editorializing while at the same time maintaining good working relationships with clients and with local government agencies?

SUGGESTED READINGS

(12) Quaal & Brown — see "Editorializing and personal attack."
(13) Rivers — chap. 16 (and follow through the "projects" section).
(15) Small — read selectively for many reference points.

Profile 4

CAN THE OLD "VAST WASTELAND" EVER BECOME VERDANT?

Station WAAA general manager Ralph Bates expressed his annoyance, concern, and most of all feeling of need for fresh thinking on the part of his staff, in a memo titled *How Can We Do A Better Job of Public Service?* The missive, addressed to all department heads, read as follows:

We try in every way we know how to be "good guys" in public service programming.

We carry all of the religious programs and "Meet the Washington People" kind of shows put out by our network.

On the local level, we follow the advice of the Everytown Council of Churches and the Ministerial Association: we use the programs and the spots they endorse; we use all of the films supplied by the Advertising Council.

We carry the announcements about using ZIP codes and mailing early for Christmas; about wearing your safety belt and not teaching your children to smoke.

Yet the effectiveness of all this is most difficult to document or to evaluate, and in truth it would seem that to be the good guy in the market is to put yourself in second place when it comes to a hard-nosed rating evaluation of station performance.

As I noted, we carry all the public service programs sent through by the network on Sunday morning and afternoon, and both rating services scratch them as "below reportable standards" in their local rating books.

Our major competitor blanks out his net's shows, and runs old movies and syndicated shows—*he* gets at least a modest rating, and sells spot announcements.

That's an easy out, but not the way for us. I'm content to see us remain No. 2 on that kind of comparative basis, *but* . . .

I continue to ask: is it not possible to construct *local* programming that would serve our community while at the same time have enough audience appeal to enable us to show up in the rating books with something more than a minimum entry that really means nothing?

Are there subjects of concern that can be amplified, maybe dramatized, for the good of the area? Do we have in our market untapped people with TV potential—local government, religious groups, volunteers in civic organizations—who would be effective on our station?

Are there, in the syndicated offerings of the religious and service groups, films or tapes that we have not explored and that might be effective here?

In short, what can we do that would remove "token" or "routine public service" from our lexicon, and give us something unique, distinctive, all our own in the market?

(And if we win an award in the doing, that won't hurt either!)

Suggested Discussion Points

Does the routine relaying of network public service programs —when available rating information indicates that there is no discernible audience viewing—have any value at all?

Would the addition (or substitution for network programs) of local public service programs be a major improvement?

Would the involvement of local religious, civic, government leaders (e.g., an advisory committee on public service programming) offer any significant improvement?

Does the local audience in truth indicate a demand for any (or all) type or types of public service programming now offered or not offered?

SUGGESTED READINGS

(1) Bleum — introduction to Part II.
(12) Quaal & Brown — chaps. 4, 5, 9 (see references to "public service broadcasting," "regulations," etc.).
(14) Roe — chap. 9.
(16) Stanley — see "regulation," etc.

Profile 5

THE DISSONANT SOUND OF A DIFFERENT DRUMMER

Another cautionary note: this is a case from a mid-1960's major market TV station experience in "experimental" programming.

If you believe that there is no longer objection on the part of the viewing audience to profanity, ethnic terms, implied prostitution, *move on to the next case study.*

But if you are aware that at least three network programs were blacked out by middle market stations during the 1976–77 season, and several more the following year . . . and that some ethnic programs and specials *never were aired* in some markets during those same periods . . . you might find this something more than a quaint document from another age!

Station WAAA is the lone independent in a four-station market of 400,000 homes. As such it enjoys fair success, with major sports, children's shows and newer movies as its staple saleable products. Sy Charles, the program director, judiciously avoided "spinning our wheels" in attempting serious competition in the network prime time program area; instead concentrated the station program highlights and supporting promotion in time periods where he sensed the best chance of gaining good audiences.

Charles took a long look at the Sunday evening schedules on the competition; decided that, "Between the built-in appeal of the action out on the Ponderosa, the dancing bears and the powerhouse movies, we don't stand a chance.

"But I am going to propose an alternative for a minority

The Dissonant Sound of a Different Drummer 125

audience segment—an evening for *culture vultures,* for people who like their opera without 'horse' in front of it and who have outgrown the Doris Day-John Wayne movie era.

"We'll build a *New York Times*-type 'Week in Review' series, and follow it with a discussion program, and then buy the Chicago Symphony miniature concert tapes, and for the main attraction we'll use the 'Play of the Week' dramatic shows from New York."

WAAA manager Ted Steiner supported the plan immediately, noting that it was a good gesture of public service as well as a program outline that might attract some advertisers who don't care to associate with the norm of TV fare—"We might possibly break even, which would be a first for the industry in itself," he grinned.

Subsequent rating reports gave indication that the plan was working: while the other stations hadn't lost any of their audience, additional homes were tuning to Charles' *culture vulture* experiment, with emphasis on the "Play of the Week" anthology dramas.

With top Broadway stars and the best of standard stage literature, the play series could scarcely be faulted. Greek tragedies, Victorian comedies, 20th century European and American writings all played well. One of the most ambitious offerings was Eugene O'Neill's *The Iceman Cometh,* with Jason Robards Jr. as Hickey, traveling salesman, reformed alcoholic and wife murderer. Because of the four-act construction and wordiness of the script it was taped in two parts, for showing on two consecutive weeks.

In advance of the first episode, Sy Charles wrote a memo to the WAAA staff under the heading of *The Sound of a Different Drummer*: "This is a strong play, and we may get some flack from the bible belt segment. For this reason we're holding the start of the show until 10 p.m., in the hope that the youngsters and the sanctimonious will be tucked away.

"Do be aware of the fact that the characters in this show are lushes to a man (and woman); as denizens of Harry Hope's combination saloon and rooming house, they live in alcoholic dreams of a tomorrow that never happens.

"As such, they use a natural vocabulary replete with profanity and ethnic terms; also the profession of the females is established without doubt.

"The first serious blast doesn't come until the play is about 30 minutes along. Pearl and Margie arrive to deliver their night's earnings to Rocky the bartender about 20 minutes later. From that point on, look out!

"I doubt that we'll have much trouble, but if you get any complaints, send 'em to me."

By the Wednesday after the Sunday showing of the first episode, it was more than evident that you didn't have to carry Lawrence Welk on your station to get cards and letters. Two baskets of mail sat in Sy's office, and the stack of phone calls recorded was several inches high.

"About two dozen nice, thoughtful, well-written letters of thanks," Charles reported to his manager, "and all the rest say that we are in league with the devil, seeking to contaminate today's youth, and that we should be put off the air!

"The phone callers use words that O'Neill would never have considered for his play. We haven't had any trouble since we accidentally ran *Medea* on Mothers' Day—and now this!"

"It isn't going to brankrupt us," Steiner said, "but you should know that two clients were pressured into withdrawing their spots from next week's second part. A few others, mostly retail stores, are holding firm, but are getting threats of boycotts if they continue to advertise with us."

"Do they know," Charles asked, "that 75% of these cards are identically worded, and were suggested from the pulpits of a major denomination on the Sunday morning *before* the show went on?"

"Sure they do. A couple of them even heard it in their own churches. But they're in business, and worried about their own public relations.

"The important point now," Steiner continued, "is that both the religion editor and the TV editor of the newspaper are pressing me for a statement—do we intend to run the second episode next Sunday as scheduled? And they won't be put off much longer."

"And I suppose that if we go ahead, they'll run a story that starts 'TV ignores public; flaunts harmful program before our youth.' Ted, don't they realize that O'Neill is the dean of modern playwrights? That he got a string of Pulitzers, and the Nobel as well?"

"Yes, of course, and I don't think they'll be quite that severe. But it won't be good. I reminded Jones at the *Star* that one of the networks had run a story about a salesman, and nobody objected—

The Dissonant Sound of a Different Drummer 127

—even said that I thought Hickey in *The Iceman* was in truth a more honest and moral character than Willie Loman in *Death of a Salesman*.

"Jones was funny about it. He said: "You've got a point—but Willie didn't hang out with the same kind of crowd!'

"In any event, Sy, Jones has a deadline this afternoon. What do we tell him?"

Suggested Discussion Points

Charles was well aware of the controversial potential of the play in his "bible belt" market; should he *not* have scheduled it in the first place?

Since Steiner isn't greatly upset over the loss of revenue, is there anything to be gained by cancelling the second episode?

Are there any useful public relations devices to be employed *in advance* of the airing of the second episode?

If the second episode is played, in what ways can the station prepare for an anticipated second round of attacks?

Finally, *should* the second episode be aired as scheduled?

SUGGESTED READINGS

(7) Friendly — selective readings under subtitle.
(12) Quaal & Brown — references under "Programming" section.
(16) Stanley — see "program content."

Profile 6

TWEAKING NOSES AND KICKING OVER CANS

The incident began the night Station WAAA news director Steve Porter nodded to a large, black-outlined card hanging behind his head, just as he closed his TV report. "You might wonder what this card with the numeral 7 on it signifies. Well, it marks the seventh straight day that Pete Marvin, publisher of our own hometown *Argus,* has had his picture on page one of his own newspaper. Congratulations and good night, Pete—will we see you tomorrow?"

The next day's paper was already set, and in the early edition the publisher was once again up front, in a Rotary club luncheon group. Porter opened his evening show by gesturing over his shoulder: "Yep, there it is—eight. But do you know that in the later edition the editor moved Pete back to the second section!

"It's only fair, though," Porter went on with a smile. "Mr. Marvin only stayed for the introduction, the picture-taking and the shrimp. Just about the time we had our TV film camera set up, he was called away."

The TV picture then dissolved to a rear view of the corpulent publisher scurrying down the back corridor of a hotel, as Porter narrated: "Why the hurry? Pete is doing a two-for-one. Having blessed his fellow Rotarians, he's now heading for another luncheon meeting—at the Town Club!"

The TV film changed to a long-lens shot of Marvin exiting through the rear door of the Town Club and jogging down an alley. "And there he goes," Porter continued, "on his way to who knows what? Certainly not yet another luncheon meeting."

Porter looked into the studio camera solemnly: "We are happy to report that the menu at the Town Club did *not* include shrimp!"

Soap opera organ music came in as Porter concluded his report: "Some people are table hoppers; Pete-the-Affable is a compulsive luncheon club joiner, it would seem. Tune in tomorrow for the next episode. Will Pete make it nine? It's Kiwanis day, so we'll look for him there—and who knows where else?"

The next morning Steve Porter was asked to attend a meeting in general manager Hal Ross's office. The room also contained a serious sales manager and an anxious promotion man.

"Steve, you've got a great thing going," Ross said, "and personally I'm getting a great chuckle out of it. Marvin is an egomaniac, and these clubs all pull him in and make him chairman of committees because they know it's the surefire way to get page one publicity in his papers. And he loves it—has his name on all the club mastheads, runs all over the place, but never has time to do anything because he's so busy.

"But you've also got a tiger by the tail. Dick says that several local retailers, our clients as well as the paper's, indicate that Marvin is furious, and that he is going to be very hard to do business with for anybody who buys us."

The sales manager nodded: "Puts us in a real bind with the advertisers who hang on the paper's goodwill for a lot of extra space—features on fashions and furnishings and recipes, for example."

"In another area," Ross said, "our network publicity people have been shut out completely on any kind of TV column space—the TV editor simply said that we are uncooperative, even negative."

"And," the promotion man added, "they either lost, or reduced, most of our listings in last night's TV page."

"Sorry to hear it," Porter answered. "But wait'll you see what we have for tonight. Ed has put together a film montage of all of those pictures for the last eight days, and we'll play the 'Stars and Stripes Forever' under it, and the narration . . ."

"Steve," Ross interrupted, "that's all good fun, but we have to take a more serious look at the situation that has developed. Bad press handling, clients clearing their throats nervously, the network worried—I know about the great traditions of press rivalry, and I do appreciate humor and satire and the twitting of the competitor. And I know that a lot of people in town are enjoying this whole thing immensely, and hang on what will happen next.

"But what we have to resolve here is the question of whether this is really in the province of television—can we afford ourselves the luxury of tweaking noses and kicking over cans, even when we know those cans are filled with a garbage the aroma of which will appeal to much of our audience?"

Suggested Discussion

There are no readings indicated for this case study, nor a set of discussion points: the query to be posed is voiced by Ross in the last paragraph—". . . what we have to resolve here is the question of whether this is really in the province of television."

PART III

Situation Statements

1

FM—FREQUENCY MODULATION OR FINE MUSIC?

The specialized electronic spectrum of FM (Frequency Modulation) has inherited a reputation for "good" music, uninterrupted program segments, few (if any) commercial messages—a pleasant sort of background "Muzak" for the home, the doctor's office and the store.

There's an assumed additional *plus* of superior sound quality —although the measurement of that sound quality as played through a three-inch speaker may be challenged.

FM in stereo has the promise of the ultimate in this concept of superiority: but who, other than the most dedicated of afficionados, is programmed to sit at the apex of two sound sources for an extended, *commercially-saleable,* period of time?

But to the important point: in recent years it has become startlingly clear that FM is *not* synonymous with "fine music." The pattern in AM radio, mass appeal, competitive radio of *sound* or *image* or *station personality* is basic to the medium: country & western, all-news, Top 40, acid or progressive rock and the rest of the standard radio formats are familiar phrases as well as sounds to the radio audience.

Why not then an FM signal in any of those formats plus a half-dozen others? Why should FM be considered a ubiquitous sandwich spread, when it could be as challenging, attention-catching, even as noisesome as the crashingest personality-laden rocker in town?

Every here and there, mostly in the country's largest markets, an FM outlet has been programmed in this direction, and with dramatic results. Ratings have shot up as Cousin Willie yelled "All you dudes catch this one" and spun the latest and the greatest, with "vintage" offerings of the Beatles and a scattering of Elvis.

Sharply-ascending ratings have a sweet aroma to managers and salesmen: *now* we can raise the rates and sell more time, maybe even national accounts—all based on that documentable audience.

So they do, and the sales curve climbs almost as sharply as the ratings chart—for a time.

But the audience that responded so favorably to the new sound, the contemporary focal point for their aural and other senses, suddenly finds a distracting noise interrupting their pleasures: *commercials,* soft and musical, loud and musical, just plain loud, grating, repetitive—in short, all of the same messages for the same products and approaching the same frequency and irritation level that caused the audience to tune away from the regular sounds of AM radio in the first place!

So the pendulum swings: the next rating period shows a decreased audience, which guarantees less commercials and more entertainment. But the station can no longer afford the hotshot program manager who came in to turn the corner, or the services of Cousin Willie and his built-in appeal to the youth audience—he's gone to an AM station for twice the money!

To Build an FM Radio: Case Study Proposition

You are in a market of seven AM radio stations, three of which garner the major share of the audience while the owners have a small part of the total. There are three TV stations; there is only a small amount of spillover from larger outside areas; mass transportation is minimal and the bulk of the working force drives to and from its employment.

There are two FM stations, one public education-financed and non-commercial: the other (which you are about to take over) a nondescript leftover from the days when it merely duplicated the AM signal of the mutual owner.

A plus for you is a recent survey which indicates that a major share of the potential audience has the technical ability to receive an FM signal: specifically there are between 65 and 70 per cent of the households in the market area with at least one radio set capable of receiving an FM signal.

That leftover FM signal now is *yours*. Is there a potential for building additional radio audience with new and different programming? Can you devise content that will switch listeners from another frequency to yours?

2

BROADCASTING IN THE PUBLIC INTEREST—YOU'D BEST TAKE CARE OF US!

Miami Beach police chief Rocky Pomerance expressed the sentiment with a sigh, somewhere in-between the political conventions of 1972: "The police can't win—they just try to lose as gracefully as possible."

Broadcasters, sans uniform but equally exposed to the public, are not far removed in position: no radio or television manager has to be reminded that above all else he is licensed to operate his fiefdom "in the public interest, convenience and necessity."

A wide variety of the body politic reminds the broadcaster in an equally wide variety of ways. Aspiring politicians and entrenched encumbents alike rumble about something called "equal time": every minority interest from the Unicycle League to the save-the-white-horse committee has a special interpretation of another something called "The Fairness Doctrine."

Challengers to the broadcaster's applied-for license renewal jog in the wings, swing from ropes just above the proscenium arch, and crouch in the orchestra pit. The florid statements of how they could do the job better range from stand-off realistic to Fantasia at peak volume: one petitioning group sees better ways of serving that local interest while earning the projected 12 per cent after-tax return for itself: another ignores the basic of salaries, overhead and the cost of operation while it simply claims that it can "Tell it like it is, right on," presumably with a camera fixed on a continuing 16-hours-a-day dialogue between militant spokespeople.

"You'd Best Take Care of Us!"

Churchmen of various denominations add to the clamor. While not particularly offering any programming of merit, they are eager and willing witnesses at any negatively-oriented hearing involving a license renewal.

Anti-church people are equally avid in watchfulness, ready to claim that "equal time" for any moment given over to religious offerings.

And there are the Boston ladies who want all commercials removed from children's shows—while at the same time asking laws that would require the broadcaster to produce expensive "quality" youth programming.

And ecology campaigners, and public land developers, and P-TA presidents and school administrators, and the ADA and the AL and the ACLU and the VFW and the DAR and all the rest— "If you are broadcasting in the public interest and you honor equal time and you know about the fairness doctrine and (implied) you want your license renewed, *you'd best take care of us!*

TAKE CARE OF US! THE CASE STUDY PROPOSITION

Subsequent studies in the text examine the specific of the Fairness Doctrine and the provisions of Section #315.

The query here is slightly different: how do *you* (station manager of WAAA) take care of *them? They* range from sincere individuals and groups with unique problems, through the middle ground of standard organizations protecting a *status quo* to local militant thrusts and on to outside pressured-and-backed agitation.

The basic question: *How do you build a solid public affairs program, both in concept and in personnel, to anticipate and to meet these pressures and demands?* And to report the costs and justification of same to your board of directors?

3

RADIO: IN A STATE OF FROZEN MOBILITY

Much is made of radio's ability to go anywhere, do anything; to reach the listener wherever he or she happens to be, and at any hour of the day or night.

Technically true. The Radio Advertising Bureau, promotional arm of the industry, has more adjectives: "Flexibility . . . instant information . . . moves to meet the unexpected . . . a constant companion . . . news as it happens . . ." and much more.

Local radio in actual practice is formatted, by the clock, by the sequence of commercials on the log, by the "brand new, original concept" of the current program manager. Little short of an earthquake, or a tidal wave licking at the studio doors, will cause that format to deviate.

Examples? The worst blizzard of a decade innundates a metropolitan area; streets impassable, schools closed, no public transportation. Yet at 7:55 a.m. the only suburban station for the hardest-hit area puts on an 11-minute tape of the mayor, talking about "the great progress of this city in the next 25 years." *Instant information, moving to meet the unexpected?* The log called for the tape—and there was only one person on duty anyway.

An absolute disaster of a commuter railroad tie-up: derailment, no trains running, a potential of 85,000 riders unable to get to work. A station with a news studio 200 feet from the railroad station where the accident happened, offers: "More commuter transportation news at 8:30 (25 minutes!) . . . and now we return to Happy Cousin Willie with the Swingin' **** Club!"

Radio: In a State of Frozen Mobility

Isolated examples perhaps. Radio doesn't make money by exerting itself in terms of emergency information for people—but it doesn't lose much either, and it can lose audience loyalty—*permanently*. An old show business story tells of Roy Rogers, seated on a rock and tuning his guitar. A messenger rushes up: "Roy, the Injuns is all to the north of yore ranch, and pore Dale is inside all alone, an' they gonna rush in . . ."

Roy grunts; goes on tuning.

Another messenger dashes up with a similar message about a marauding band to the south; another to the east and then to the west.

Each time Roy grunts.

The four breathless messengers cry out: "Roy, watcha gonna do?"

Rogers stands, adjusts his gun belt, and they look on admiringly. "I'm gonna go up thar an' pick off them varmints from all directions, one at a time," he mutters.

Then he picks up his guitar: "But furst I'm gonna sing a little song!"

Nonsense story? Certainly—but with a measure of seriousness when applied to this subject. Much of the above is unfair to the good service done by radio stations in many markets—but most of these services come from the fortunate situation of a combined radio and television operation, where adequate news staff and a fleet of mobile units can move to meet an emergency situation.

But the purely radio, 12-person staff outlet can't do much other than "sing a little song" when a community disaster strikes. The jock on duty, who unlocked the door, turned the transmitter on, ripped from the news wire, opened the day, can do little other than follow the log. Until relief comes in to take the messages of school closings, train delays, blocked streets, weather warnings—that jock can only follow the instructions in the book in front of the mike.

So the 11-minute message of good cheer from the mayor goes on as scheduled—if only to give the jock time to get the hard news of the moment together.

But the situation doesn't say much for that *flexibility, instant information* promotional language.

Adequate personnel is an obvious answer. But the very disaster conditions that cause the emergency problem most likely delay, or even prevent, that back-up personnel from getting to the studio.

. . .

To Unfreeze for Mobility: The Case Study Proposition

Hurricanes, tornados, crop-damaging frost, road-icing, earthquake rumblings, high winds—the potential disasters that threaten various parts of the country offer local radio its best shot at truly public service. And it's a responsible shot that no other medium can command. *How do you anticipate this, and what standby provisions do you make?*

4

FAIR IS FOUL, FOUL IS FAIR

The Federal Communication Commission's revised procedural manual titled "Public and Broadcasting," dated September 5, 1974, contains all that is current and legal under the heading of *Fairness Doctrine*.

One place where the words may conveniently be found is in Appendix *B* of *The Broadcast Industry: An Examination of Major Issues*—#16 in the list of referenced texts.

This is a particularly rewarding document to research, because it is the report of a seminar convened by the New York-based International Radio and Television Society, Inc., mixing educators in mass communications with leading executives from the commercial broadcast industry. The seminar program was formed from the pattern of the first edition of *Case Studies in Broadcast Management,* and this writer had opportunity to serve on the committee formulating the content. Thus the case study in that text: "Regulation: A Full Nelson, or a Stranglehold?" actually anticipates *this* case study—and offers a wide variety of opinions from the sides of what appears to be an octagon-shaped fence.

That faculty-industry seminar painted with a wide brush, to incorporate *License Renewal, Equal Time* and *Counter or Non-Advertising*. That these are gray and overlapping areas is evident in the pages of discussion: it is most strongly suggested here that the *Fairness Doctrine* is more than enough for a subject in itself.

In another referenced text, *The Media Environment* (#17), authors Stanley and Steinberg include in their chapter on Broadcasting Law the all-encompassing, definitive review of the obfuscated legalese that is "The Fairness Doctrine." It would be futile, even unfair, to extract from it here. *Read it:* it tells the whole story.

But Drs. Stanley and Steinberg can enjoy the privilege of ending the chapter with a possible projection to the future plus a trio of question marks: "Is the FCC's regulation of broadcast content consistent with the prevailing constitutional standards regarding obscene and indecent material? Do FCC programming standards restrict adults to broadcast expression deemed appropriate for children or easily offended adults? Does the FCC employ rigorous safeguards to ensure that constitutionally protected expression is not curtailed?"

Good questions, but where are the answers for the station manager? For starters, here are the discussion points on *Fairness Doctrine* posed for the faculty-industry seminar described above:

> "If we must live under the Fairness Doctrine, who is to be the final arbiter of what is fair? Can a national standard of fairness be established or do local situations make this an impossible task? If a subject were to be labeled editorial or commentary, who is to make the final judgment in the event that there are several seemingly valid requests for equal time?"

How Do I Handle It? The Case Study Proposition

"I'm the station manager—what if this happens to me?". . . is the case study. Read and read, and *anticipate*. What *do* you do—not in response to but in anticipation of—your editorial supporting one candidate or attacking another?

Or your news reporting of a contested issue before your city council? Or the exposure on one of your talk shows of a citizen with a partisan axe to grind?

Suggested readings: under the *Fairness Doctrine* entries, see readings in ##2, 4, 6, 7, 9, 12, 16, 17 and 19.

5

THE FEMALE ANCHORPERSON: CAN THE INDUSTRY AFFORD THE MILLION-DOLLAR BABY?

> Amazon, applied to female warriors, masculine women and women of outstanding physical development and courage, derives from a mythical race of warrior women. They were associated with the territory adjoining the river Thermodon in Cappadocia.
>
> *Cecil Hunt. Philosophical Library, New York, 1949*

In the minds of many male traditionalists in broadcast news, the value of the female of the species as a professional newsperson was fully demonstrated during the 1976 Democratic convention. President Carter had been selected as the candidate, and the females of the Carter family—all three generations—were in a box overlooking the convention floor.

An intrepid electronic reporter, mike in hand, thrust her way into the box and said: "Hello, Amy. I'm Leslie Stahl of CBS News. Amy, do you have a message for the youth of America?"

And eight-year-old Miss Carter, more than a little tired, had a message that was fully worthy of the question. She said: "Huh?"

(It was also the final straw for Rosalynn Carter, who announced that the child was being withdrawn from all press interviews.)

The real spotlight on women in the broadcast news profession of course came when Barbara Walters bolted her longtime chair on the early morning NBC "Today" show to assume the weighty title of "co-anchorperson" with veteran Harry Reasoner on ABC's early evening network news. The rumored million dollar contract was the news key: "Nobody's worth a million bucks a year to read the news!"

And even though it was pointed out that the seven-figure contract included a substantial number of special features and other assignments, the "million dollar baby" phrase came up again and again.

The role of the female in journalism—specifically in hard news reporting—is hardly a new one: both in print and in the broadcast media there have been and are formidable distaff journalists and photojournalists who have reported nationally and worldwide, often topping their male competitors.

It was only in mid-1976 when the *happening* (or maybe threat) of a female newscaster making the protean jump to the evening network news became in itself *news,* that the industry and the nation came to attention and took sides.

One broadcast trade paper said that "If her (Barbara Walters) presence on the ABC early news lifts the Nielsens one point, the money will be worth it."

Well it did. But the competition came up too, for whatever it's worth.

But in the careful buildup of a news interviewer, Barbara Walters was also seen in in-depth special interviews with Bob Hope, Frank Sinatra, Fidel Castro, and many others. Remember: a lot of hard work, and a good part of that reputed million dollar-baby contract.

An editorial note. I have not referred to Barbara Walters as *Miss*—because she is married and divorced and doesn't travel under those labels—nor as *Ms.* or *Walters.* (See the New York *Times Manual of Style and Usage.*)

But what about the local TV station? Or radio station? Do you, the station manager, employ a woman simply because you feel some pressures to put a female voice into local news? Is she then a news reader or a journalist? Top schools in mass communications are turning out female as well as male personnel in a wide variety of talents: many with superior vocal skills as well as abilities in the usual camera operation, switching and the like.

POTENTIAL FEMALE ANCHORPERSON: THE CASE STUDY PROPOSITION

In Station WAAA-TV, as manager, you have local pressures for a better female presence in your news and public affairs programming. With your news director and your public affairs director, how do you resolve this?

6

GENERAL MOTORS, JESUS, AND WHO PRESSURES WHOM?

The offering by NBC was simple and dramatic: "Three years in the making, Franco Zeffirelli's production of *Jesus of Nazareth* was filmed in Morocco, Tunisia and Rome. It is an ITC-RAI production which will be telecast on NBC-TV on two successive Sundays, April 3 and April 10. To insure authenticity, outstanding authorities from the Protestant, Catholic, Jewish and Moslem religions served as religious technical advisors."

The cast was formidable: young Robert Powell as Jesus; with Anne Bancroft, Ernest Borgnine, Claudia Cardinale, James Earl Jones, James Mason, Laurence Olivier, Anthony Quinn, Peter Ustinov and Olivia Hussey arbitrarily selected to demonstrate the roster's quality.

The program was scheduled for two consecutive three-hour screenings on the NBC-TV network: 8–11 p.m. on Palm Sunday and Easter, 1977. (It so ran.)

And the bankroller of the entire project: General Motors. But the conviction of that GM support, with a close to $5 million investment in the three-year project, came to a close suddenly, after religious pressure groups had launched a campaign against the program—a campaign that urged boycotting GM products.

The *Jesus of Nazareth* director had been quoted as saying that "the public is going to be annoyed that I am destroying their myths, emphasizing Jesus' humanity at the expense of his divinity." Fundamentalist religious groups, led by Dr. Bob Jones, Southern

General Motors, Jesus, and Who Pressures Whom? 147

Baptist and the president of Bob Jones University, responded by calling on believers in Christ's divinity to "make their protest known" to GM "both verbally and by spending their automobile dollars elsewhere."

An Associated Press wire feed quoting Zeffirelli to the effect that Christ would be de-mythified evidently first triggered fundamentalist reaction.

But at this stage, nobody had seen the film!

GM pulled out. A spokesman said because of "the sensitivity of the subject and the conflict inherent in commercial sponsorship of a program on the life of Christ." After three years.

Next was the announcement that "Procter and Gamble" (#1 TV advertiser in 1976) "Becomes GM's Savior" (#4 advertiser). The buy-up of the original GM investment was rumored to be at a bargain price. *Variety* reported candidly that General Motors had "chickened out" under pressure from fundamentalist religious leaders and groups.

Net result: *Jesus of Nazareth* reached a staggering 90 million viewers in its first offering; close to 90 per cent of that figure for its second week.

Presumably—and deservingly—the pick-up sponsor, Procter and Gamble, received adequate response.

The program received lavish critical acclaim. The secular press lauded it; communications leaders of many Christian denominations lauded the production; it was most certainly destined to go around again and again—and the requests for use of the films in various non-TV educational situations were almost instantaneous.

Commercially, *Variety* pointed out that 37 minutes were added to the over-all program to include Procter and Gamble commercials—but there was little criticism.

WHAT DO I DO? THE CASE STUDY PROPOSITION

What if that network problem spills over? What if you, the local market operator, get caught in this bind?

What we have looked at is a network problem. But the pressure groups that set out to oppose the airing of that particular two-part program also forced themselves on many local stations—without a screening of what they opposed. Suppose the local General Motors distributor-dealer is threatened with a boycott, and you are his major advertising voice in the market? What contacts do you have with, and what options do you have with, your network—to relieve a difficult situation, with a minimum of adverse publicity?

7

YOUR HORSE FOR MY COW: BARTER

"Barter is as old as time!" says a broadcast executive. "And that's not radio or TV time—it's time as far back as history goes."

Your horse for my cow was a common concept in areas where real money was tight, suspect or even non-existent. Units of exchange have always taken a variety of forms: livestock, produce, furs, gunpowder, slaves, diamonds.

There is a tradition in our family that one Pennsylvania ancestor, noted for the quality of the whiskey that he developed in small kegs, was hailed when he drove horse and wagon to the county market with a load of "Onkel Gottlieb's Finest." Not only did those miniature barrels of the Finest trade off well for family necessities: Gottlieb was in most cases able to bring home some bolts of fine cloth for dresses and draperies, a jug of French brandy, and an ostrich plume for Grandma's church hat.

A fair exchange is no bargain? Not so: all sides were satisfied; they got 110 per cent from their point of view.

Barter in broadcasting has a long history. It reached a high point in radio (before being shot down by the Sherman Anti-Trust Act interpretations) when major market network-owned radio stations had merchandising plans that traded spot announcement time to food chains for preferred store display space for their food advertisers.

Under such plans as "Chain Lightning" and "The Market Basket," A&P, Safeway, Jewel, Red Owl, Grand Union and the rest earned most of their radio advertising by the expedient of providing window display space, end-of-aisle dumps, wider shelf space, special print advertising space in neighborhood shopping flyers and the like.

As television developed, specialized barter companies came into being, in a pattern from trade-offs on the sides of delivery trucks to illuminated "talking" signs over New York's Times Square. Some of the catalogs of these barter groups were and are as dazzling as the Nieman-Marcus Christmas catalog: you give us x thousand dollars credit in TV spots for our customers, with an audience of y thousand viewers weekly—and then pick from the catalog what you need for prizes for your giveaway shows and your Christmas parties.

Tempting? An absentee radio station owner finally went to his property in a small Texas market to investigate why, although the books balanced favorably and the auditor's report was circumspect, he had no profit. He found that the manager and his wife had his-and-hers Jaguars and Comanches—all legitimately traded out with a barter company—but very little cash flow. (He found a more cash-minded manager.)

TV stations have traded out transmitters and other engineering equipment, office equipment, fleets of station wagons—even in one case a Rolls-Royce.

Barter and its first cousin, *timebanking,* are the forms to be contemplated here. "Barter has become complex, confusing and computerized," says the March 14, 1977 *Television/Radio Age.* "It is being re-formed, refined and reshaped and is a growing force in TV syndication, with most major (advertising) agencies either in it, back to it or moving into it."

What does this mean to you the station manager? Somebody invests in and produces a TV show—let's say for openers 20 weekly 30-minute episodes. Possibly each program stands on its own; or maybe it's a series format, with a husband-wife or boy friend-girl friend focus.

In whatever form, it's attractive—even though production values are modest—and has the potential of filling some half-hour of your local programming, daytime or early evening prime fringe time.

Contrary to buying rights from one of the syndication companies, this is yours, *free* and *exclusive in your market,* with the opportunity to sell three, maybe four, 60-second openings to most advertisers.

Most but not *any and all:* the program distributor retains the rights to at least two one-minute openings per program—and possibly the billboards as well. Depending on the attractiveness of the shows (meaning ratings points earned) the distributor may also look for contracted *timebanking,* earning dollar brownie points not just within the program but for use in other parts of the station's unbought daily log.

. . .

WHISKEY FOR FEATHERS? THE CASE STUDY PROPOSITION

The proposition to you as station manager: Do you want to. can you see advantages in, trading off *your air*—mostly in 30-minute segments—for barter programming, and maybe timebanking of spot time as well? Tempting and teasing: also a way to go around the traditional percentage contract with your national spot representation firm.

There's lots available, and apparently more to come: what to do with it? Some 1977 titles: "This is Baseball," "Speak with Suzy," "It's Tough to Make It in This League," "The Magic Show of Mark Wilson," "Sha Na Na."

Two basic questions: (1) What bearing will this have or your relationship with your sales representation firm? and (2) Does the barter programming have the quality to compete with syndicated off-network re-runs that may be playing against you on your competition?

8

ENHANCING THE NEWS: ETHICAL OR "BANG-BANG!"

A midwest radio station had a brief fling at enhancing its news-on-the-hour with sound effects: when a police chase was reported, it fed in sirens and squealing tires in the background; for an alleged shooting, a few rounds of staccato submachine gun fire; for a bombing, an earth-rumbling explosion.

All this from a one-man news desk plus an adept engineer.

And all, of course, very much in violation of the NAB code and of FCC directives. And of good common sense, *if* we have to fall back on that!

Now that practice didn't even last out the rating period, once the competitors cried out to the Federal Communications Commission's regional office.

That was fact. Satire sometimes cuts deep. A *New Yorker* cartoon showed a TV production studio, with eight people assembled side-by-side behind a broad desk labeled "Action News." The *anchorperson* is saying this: "We'll be back in a minute with Harlan Harris's Sports Extra, Jules Bernmeier and the weather, Jimmy Cunningham's Entertainment Plus, Judith Enright's Fashion Notes, Grady O'Toole's Celebrity Interview, Maria Dellage's Budget Center, Murray Vaughn's Mr. Fix-It Shop, and me, Biff Brogan, with a note on the news."

NBC newsman Carl Stokes, former Cleveland mayor, said *yes* when, as a member of a panel before the New York chapter of the National Academy of Television Arts and Sciences, the question was: "Is TV news *news?*"

Enhancing the News

Stokes continued: "TV news is indeed news—when it is not being entertainment, a sex-appeal contest among anchormen or a headline service."

Ray Miller, KPRC-TV, Houston vice president for news and public affairs, had a stern message for his audience at a broadcast meeting in May, 1977: "I believe that some people in the television business believe that television news is for people who don't want to be bothered with the news. And this is what has created the demand for gimmicks and window-dressing in our business. It is more important to have an audience for the news program than it is to have news in the news program."

Can news reportage on the electronic media—without prostituting itself in the siren boom-boom manner, red blazers and Hollywood make-up—enhance itself with sound, with intelligent commentary, with saved film footage?

Consider this example from WCBS-TV (channel 2) New York . . .

On Friday, April 1, 1977, the management of the New York Jets announced that veteran quarterback Joe Willy Namath had been placed on waivers. Which meant what? Unable to make a successful trade to bolster their faltering offense, the Jets freed Joe to bargain for himself.

The news was not unexpected. Broadway Joe, flamboyant QB for the Jets, had a swinger reputation that couldn't stop. Off-Broadway and on the gridiron his daytime performance was sporadic: like the little girl in the nursery rhyme, when he was good he was very good, and when he was bad he was horrid.

When he was good was enough times, despite recurring knee injuries and operations, to mark him as one of the greatest quarterbacks of all time, from college days through NFL championships to the Superbowl.

But 1976 had been a frustrating year: rushed, blitzed, intercepted, second-guessed—*bad news*.

That's all routine sports news. Where does the very special expertise of electronic journalism come in? This way (which nobody ever mentioned in the critical press that reviews so much of TV news efforts) . . .

In the closing credits of the April 1 WCBS-TV New York 11:00–11:30 p.m. news period, and under the crawl of credits for editors, writers, technical staff et al, they ran a film montage of Broadway Joe's worst moments of the 1976 season: smashed, blitzed, intercepted.

The genius of it all was this: they played a nostalgic record of "Give My Regards to Broadway, Remember Me to Herald Square," etc. No announcement; no rubbing it in. You either caught it or you didn't.

If you did, it caught you right in the gut. If you didn't, you went to get a beer before the late movie.

But if you did, you had to say to yourself that somebody down there was busting a gut in trying to make news reportage more than *here's what happened today-weather-sports.*

Enhancing the News: The Case Study Proposition

What's your news image; can you upgrade it? That, very simply, is the case study question. *How,* honoring ethical concepts of the over-all umbrella of "Here's the news tonight," can you give your station's image the *plus* that causes the listener or viewer to think "How intelligent, how clever, how thoughtful—those are my kind of people. I want to continue to hear and see what they will do next!"

HE 8689 .8 C58 1978

MAR 14

JAN 11 1991
OCT 04 1991